A Scheme of Study for Country Violin Students

AND

Occasional Papers

BY

L. HENDERSON WILLIAMS

1914

INTRODUCTION.

FROM personal experience and through hearsay I have been aware for a long time that there are many would-be violinists, scattered thinly in remote and inaccessible places, who are unable for lack of money, opportunity, or leisure, to obtain teaching. The instrument is dear to them: they handle it constantly with clumsy and timorous affection. But, alas! dear Lady Disdain will not yield to them her sweetness. To all but the initiated she is unresponsive, cold, or, perhaps, by turns shrewish and distraught. Yet, love a fiddle once and you love it always—kind or unkind, complaisant or perverse.

Something, then, must be conceived to help these people so far as it may be done from a distance and through the medium of print. For a long time I turned it over in my mind and this Scheme of Study has been the result of the turning—a very tentative and imperfect scheme, yet one which I venture to hope may not be altogether useless.

As well as those who are entirely self-taught, there are players who manage to get a few good lessons during holidays, or at other infrequent intervals. It is presumable that the teacher will lay down a course of study for such pupils to be pursued in the interval between lessons. But the individual pupil may either surpass the limits of the teacher's estimate of his powers, or he may not reach it; in either case he may be able to glean something from the present course, which is in no case offered as complete, but only supplementary to personal instruction whenever it is obtainable.

In order to carry out this idea and make it of the utmost practical value, I have selected two sets of studies by different writers, and in totally contrasted spirit, namely, Kreutzer's "Forty Studies" (Forty-two in Peters' Edition), and Léonard's "Twenty-four *Études Classiques*," Op. 21. These I propose to take, two or three at a time, analyzing and discussing them from every point of view likely to be of interest to the learner. Kreutzer is invaluable from the technical point of view; Léonard appeals both to the intellect and power of interpretation.

As well as the studies, some purely finger and bowing exercises should be practised; the time and energy expended on them to be proportionate to the physical capacity of the player. As much harm as good—in fact, more—is done by excess of muscular exercise unwisely directed; but, roughly speaking, those violinists with comparatively thick, broad hands, will derive much more benefit from strenuous exertion than those whose hands are of slighter, narrower build, and whose sinews are more liable to be strained thereby. Schradieck, Wilhelmj, Kayser, and Wohlfahrt, have presented us with excellent examples of this sort of work. Sevcik I do not recommend without personal tuition ; he presents too many possibilities of error to the uninitiated student.

That very important matter, adjustment of the individual members—hands, arms, chin, shoulders, etc.— to the instrument can only be touched very generally, in negative rather than positive terms. Those who have had lessons will have been taught to hold the instrument after the school of their professors, and should not vary their mode of handling either violin or bow without good reason. Nevertheless, such reminders as occur throughout the course of the Scheme in reference to particular bowings or positions are so general and adaptable as to work harmoniously with the rules of most accepted schools. But to those who have not been taught at all, or are aware that they have not followed very reliable guides, it is necessary to offer a few preliminary warnings and suggestions which may be skipped by players more fortunately circumstanced.

L. H. W.

May, 1914.

CONTENTS

A SCHEME OF STUDY FOR COUNTRY VIOLIN STUDENTS.

		PAGE
PRELIMINARY	.. ..	1
LESSON I.	.. ..	3
LESSON II.	.. ..	8
LESSON III.	.. ..	13
LESSON IV.	.. ..	19
LESSON V.	.. ..	25
LESSON VI.	.. ..	29
LESSON VII	.. ..	35
LESSON VIII.	.. ..	40
LESSON IX.	.. ..	45
LESSON X.	.. ..	50
LESSON XI.	.. ..	54
LESSON XII	.. ..	58

OCCASIONAL PAPERS ON VIOLIN MATTERS.

	PAGE
On Playing at Sight	65
Bad Habits Incidental to Child-Violinists	68
On Musical Ideals	70
On Consistency	73
On "First Appearances"	76
On Keeping up the Interest	79
The Dull Pupil	82
On Fingering	85
On Memorising Studies	88
The Student's Fiddle	92
On Teachers – Some Portraits	95
On Holidays	98
On Accompanists	101
Good Taste in Music	104
The Importance of Bowing	108
On Originality	112
On Waste of Time	116
On Accuracy	120
On Sundry Abuses	124
On Very Small Matters	129

CONTENTS.

	PAGE
Violinists—Solo and Orchestral	133
On Musical Examinations	137
The Formation of Musical Style	141
On Opportunities	146
On Weak Sight and Hearing	150
On Characteristics of the Violin	154
On Making a Connexion	158
On Some Professional Difficulties	162
On Keeping Good Company	167

A Scheme of Study for Country Violin Students.

PRELIMINARY.

DON'T droop or hunch. Hold the neck of the fiddle level with the chin. If tired, sit down to practise and rest fiddle-head on edge of properly raised violin music stand or some article of furniture adjusted to correct height.

Don't clutch the instrument with the left hand; control it between the forefinger joint nearest the palm and the upper cushion of the thumb, but let the left jaw-bone and the collar-bone (padded if necessary) do the supporting work.

Let the left-hand palm and wrist hang except when position playing, and the tips of the fingers stop the strings firmly.

Keep the whole upper part of the body flexible rather than tense.

Hold the bow in the right hand as loosely as is compatible with safety.

Hold it close to the nut (where the hair is fixed) the tip of the thumb close to the nail being set underneath about between the first and second finger tips, but rather nearer the second.

Arrange the four fingers on the stick with the knuckles slightly slanting up towards the point. Graduate the

B

amount of finger in contact from little more than the nail-tip of the little finger to almost the whole first joint (slantwise) of the forefinger.

Remember that the position of the fingers and hand must alter with the portion of the bow being used; hence the necessity for absolute flexibility. The thumb joint, in particular, will describe a much less acute outward angle when the bow is drawn to the point and the forefinger and second finger will slope more upward.

The aim is that the bow should keep in contact with a particular portion of the gut (strings) rather than that the fingers should keep any fixed or rigid position on the bow.

W. B. means "whole bow"—from nut to point. Never scrabble with a little bit in the middle.

H. B. means "half bow" usually from nut to centre or point to centre.

Point and nut are *definite* not *approximate* terms.

Keep the bow hair level on the strings unless desirous to play extra softly. *Then* slant stick away from the body.

Don't play softly until you have learnt to produce a full round tone.

Practise scales for the sake of tone as well as tune.

Find out exactly that distance from the bridge that yields the best tone—slightly lower on the deeper strings —and keep the bow moving there; don't let it choose its own road but use the forefinger as man at the wheel.

Don't forget to learn the rhythmical values of the different note-shapes as well as their pitch and locality.

Aim at beauty and be intolerant of anything less.

Be patient with yourself.

LESSON I.

START practising always by getting the fingers into good working order: the time devoted to this must, of course, be proportionate to the duration of the whole. Scales or arpeggios do not take the place of finger exercises, because each represents only one kind of motion, they should be considered as a separate branch.

Schradieck's "Technical Violin School," Part I., is perhaps the most generally applicable to the average run of violinists, as affording steady and regulated finger exercise without any undue strain on mind or muscles. Exercises Nos. 1-24 are very simple, but not therefore to be despised. The little finger should be brought down as forcibly as possible—with more force, in fact, than the others—in order to neutralize its natural weakness. Keep the wrist well out from the neck in order to give the fingers their proper arch and fall. Memorize every passage, *in anything*, Schradieck included, in which a difficulty or uncertainty occurs. I cannot impress this too strongly upon all violinists who are anxious to succeed.

To turn to the Studies. We shall not always find it advisable to keep to the order in which they are grouped in the book, and the first of the Kreutzer volume is omitted for the present.

No. 2 is one of the most useful little studies extant. To begin with, it is so short that it can very easily be memorized, and being so similar in rhythmical style throughout, it lends itself admirably to the illustration of almost all kinds of bowing.

B 2

It is better to practise it at first in quite moderate time, using smooth half bows, first from middle to point, afterwards from nut to middle. There is much repetition of figure in it, so it will not be difficult to memorize —and without memorizing it will not afford half the benefit. The bow must be evenly balanced in changing strings, particularly from the ninth bar. It will incline to be jerky, almost missing odd notes, if the tendency is not remembered and counteracted. Single notes on a change of string present the danger. Great evenness of tone and touch should be maintained throughout, and the alterations of position accomplished inaudibly. Make sure that the top note in the last bar gets fair play. With regard to the bowings: not more than two per day should be taken as a rule. But we shall return to them from time to time.

The chief characteristic of No. 3 is repetition; repetition of phrases at a different interval and of regular sets of fingering. The first group of eight notes is followed by similar groups, each time falling a third, till end of third bar; and the group with which the fourth bar commences is repeated till middle of twelfth bar, the only variable thing being the bowing. This is, therefore, easy to remember. At bar 10 the student begins to shift, and the second finger, which has just played G, must slide on the string up to A, while the fourth finger falls on C. This applies equally to the rest of the passage until the second half of bar 12 is reached, when the first finger becomes immediately responsible for the intonation of each descending shift. The group beginning on the last two notes of bar 13 implies an awkward leap to fourth position on A string, and will need to be practised several times, without break, in succession to the preceding group on E string. Do not fail to play the final arpeggio in the second position. The things to be aimed at in this study are accuracy of tune and accuracy and neatness of bowing. The bow should be applied at the neighbourhood of the point throughout. Rather less

than a quarter should be used for the slurs, even in slow
playing, and for the staccato, only so much as can be
manipulated from the wrist alone. The varied bowings
are preferably postponed.

As a preparation for No. 4, the student is recommended to experiment with the bowing at first on a
single repeated note. Stop the note C on A string and
proceed as follows, starting the first down-bow about
four inches from the point :—

taking care to keep strict time, and to separate each
fraction of the up-bow staccato as if it were a scrap of
paper snipped off sharply with a pair of scissors. There
must on no account be a *tail* of sound between the notes,
which is caused by uneven pressure on the stick of the
bow, and the movement must be actuated by tiny jerks
from the right first finger and thumb with an absolutely
flexible wrist. Play as it were from the finger-tips, and
you will find, after the bowing is mastered, no further
difficulty with the study. But this bowing is usually
found to be difficult, particularly to those who have not
.acquired a sufficiently free wrist. The smaller the
portion of bow used the better, even in the longest
runs ; and it will be advisable to take half, starting from
the middle, rather than a whole bow on the opening
crotchet of each bar. When neatly and clearly executed
this style of bowing has a peculiarly dainty and bright
effect.

Léonard, No. 1, makes demand not only on the more
practical side of the musician's intelligence, that which
is concerned primarily with fingerings and bowings, but
on the student's power of translating printed notes into
living music, of understanding and expressing the underlying motive of varying rhythms and tonalities. These

are studies of temperament rather than of technique, and must be treated accordingly. No. 1, in *March* style, is broad and dignified, but never pompous or blatant in manner. The staccato crotchets must not be "dry" (*i.e.*, too short and hard), but played with swift, straight bow-strokes to give them the necessary brightness and clearness. In the triple and quadruple double stopping only the minims are to be sustained, the other notes being struck in acciaccatura fashion, but together, not as three separate notes. The triplet passages must be played smoothly, and connected unbrokenly with the following third or octave ; this will need considerable practice. The melody beginning on the forty-fourth bar requires a judicious broadening of tone on the second (syncopated) beat, and as each phrase really begins on the second and ends on the first beat, that first, as the final of the phrase, must be played softly and delicately.

As regards fingering :—The phrase of four crotchets starting on the last beat of bar 34 must be played entirely in the fourth position, the following phrase in the third, and the last in the second. The triplet passages beginning on the last beat of bar 38 are to be similarly fingered. Bars 49 and 51 contain examples of what is known as "false fingerings," and the whole of this passage is rather difficult to inexperienced players to stop in tune. In bars 54 and 55 the flat before the B has been unfortunately omitted in some copies ; the student should mark it in before practising if necessary. In bars 68—9, take the final and first thirds in the fourth position ; the same applies to bars 70—1. In the passage beginning on bar 89, sustain the lower note of the octave with full, sonorous tone. The note F in first chord of bar 94 is played by extension of fourth finger on A string.

Throughout the study, breadth and purity of tone should be displayed as well in the double stopping as in the single ; the time should be exact except where phrasing or sentiment plainly indicates modification, and the finals of all phrases and *motifs* should be distinctly but delicately executed. The student will find the perfecting of this study a pleasurable if not always simple task.

Having taken a little recreation, I return to the practical wisdom of Kreutzer. No. 5, which is a very straightforward study, may, with advantage, be practised with any of the first nine alternative bowings. I should recommend that it be played at first with half bows, slowly and evenly, taking care to stop firmly and well in tune. The student should need no advice as to how to set about memorising it by this time; I shall leave him to find out the landmarks for himself. If he has sufficient knowledge of harmony to recognise the modulations it will be a great help; in fact, it is practically a necessary knowledge for all serious violinists; but it would be impossible to deal with the subject in these short papers.

As regards pieces, the choice must be left to the individual, as the writer is, of course, quite in the dark as to his particular tastes and capacities; but he is recommended in all cases to select those of a less degree of technical difficulty than his studies in order that he may be able to devote himself to the spirit rather than to the letter of the music.

LESSON II.

THE first five of Group 2 in Schradieck's exercises are designed mainly to strengthen the weak third finger, and care must be taken to hold the second finger firmly and not let the pitch become sharper whilst extending the third for the harmonic second. If this is mastered, less difficulty will be experienced in extending the little finger later on. The fourth exercise of Group 3 will be found to be an excellent test of both right and left hand efficiency. The last four semiquavers of the first bar will illustrate what I mean, as, if the bow is not carefully controlled just there, it is very apt to miss the strings altogether. This exercise might well be selected for daily practice by students with little spare time. This Group is particularly recommended to the student's attention.

Kreutzer, No. 6, comes next on our list of studies. First, as regards the bowing : if the student is not very familiar with three-octave scales it will be advisable to practise from bar 19 to the end, at all events for the first half-dozen times, in ordinary legato bowing, so as to make sure not only of the tune, but of the quality of tone in the upper notes. They must be firmly stopped ; otherwise they will sound harsh or muffled ; and if the height of the bridge, set of the fingerboard, etc., are not exactly correct, more difficulty will be experienced in doing this. The student is strongly recommended to have his violin overhauled by an expert (*i.e.*, some firm whose name is sufficiently well-known to be a guarantee) before beginning a serious course of study. A few shillings spent in this way may save an infinity of small worries and perplexities later on.

If the fingers are very broad at the tips it may be found necessary, in extreme positions, to move one in order to get a succeeding semitone perfectly in tune. This must be left to the discretion of the individual, but fingers should not be lifted without good reason as success depends largely on definiteness of stopping. The *Martelé* bowing should be maintained throughout as soon as the student is acquainted with the successions of fingering, but the directions given at the head of the study, "with firm hard stroke," must not be imagined to mean a dry, gritty scratch, such as I have more than once heard unimaginative pupils maintain apparently without a qualm! No, the "hardness" must be like that of a polished brilliant, not like the action of a worn-out pen or a door on a sandy threshold; and the "firmness" includes regulation of length of stroke as well as evenness of pressure and relaxation. The only awkward passage occurs in the last line where the note G is pitched first with third and afterwards with second finger on A string immediately following the open E. The note must be gripped, not felt for.

No. 7 is concerned only with acquiring a correct balance of the bow in crossing strings. The fingering given has reference to this only, and is not to be taken as a guide to octave-playing under ordinary circumstances. Practise the bowing first on D and A strings with movement solely from the wrist; then on D and E, and finally with G and E strings, stirring the elbow as little as possible, as a violent movement causes the bow to jump and miss the note. Always start with the wrist at the proper level for the two inner strings and the subsequent variation to either side will not be too extreme.

No. 8 hardly calls for comment. It is a useful and tuneful study but perfectly straightforward if the fingering is faithfully followed. In bars 28 and 29 both fingers should be shifted together for the octave, and this applies to all ordinary octave playing. The little finger should be slipped cleanly (neither lifted nor drawled) from the last stopped note to the harmonic of the final arpeggi. The alternative bowings may be practised with benefit, but the first (ordinary legato, with the upper third of the bow in moderate time) is the best to begin with.

We will now turn to Léonard, No. 2. This is a peaceful, meditative movement suggestive of Sabbath stillness in a sylvan country, green undulating plains, bird-haunted hedgerows, and hollows where cattle stand knee-deep amid the reeds that fringe slow-moving waters. The fact that it is written in E flat may affright some unenterprising violinists, but let me reassure them; it really is not difficult. The main consideration, after tune, is tone; purity and equality in the sustained semibreves and the avoidance of awkward jerks in moving the bow from string to string whilst the left hand is also moving to a difficult interval. This is likely to occur, if the player is not careful, between the last and first beats of bars 13—14, and similarly in bars 20 and 29—30. Careful attention must be paid to gradation of tone and phrasing.

Léonard, No. 3, is the most complete contrast that can be imagined to the preceding. If one were asked to give a concrete analogy one might suggest Monday morning, a frosty sky, and a mood of extra strenuousness; or a mental spring-cleaning with particular attention to all the out-of-the-way corners. It is a study in syncopation, and any student who is inclined to be lax in the matter of time, or whose eye is not yet trained to grasp the meaning of apparently complicated grouping, will do well to look silently over a few bars, counting eight quavers, before he begins to play. The rhythmical effect of the first and second bars should be identical; the first bar is only written dissimilarly in order to show how the rest of the study is intended to *sound* by means of bowing and accent—*i.e.*, with an abrupt and clipped accent on the final half of the syncopated note. Beware of the alteration of rhythm commencing in bar 4 and continuing to bar 11. From bars 12 to 22, keep the finger stationary on the repeated note, and make sure that the extreme notes in bars 31, 33 and 35 are clearly and neatly touched. In bars 60 as well as 61 the B flat must be taken by extension. Play throughout with energy and precision.

I hope, though I have not hitherto mentioned it, that the student has not neglected scale and arpeggio practice graded according to his ability? Mr. Hans Wessely's book is the most comprehensive that I know of on these matters; but the pupil should begin with the scales and arpeggios in two octaves (page 38, Augener's edition, No. 5686) instead of with those in three, even if he feels quite capable of attacking the latter. There are little differences in fingering peculiar to the two-octave group which are liable to disconcert a player who has neglected them if he meets with a succession of such passages to be played at sight in the orchestra or elsewhere.

Kreutzer, No. 9, is sometimes found fatiguing, but it is well worth mastering not only because it strengthens the muscles according as the fingers become accustomed to their work, but because it familiarizes the eye with quick changes of position and fixes the ensuing fingering in the mind by means of repetition. Pupils should note that it opens in the second position, and the tone should be even and not thin throughout the long bow-strokes. The tune in bars 16 and 29 may require attention, and the same from bars 40—44. Bars 80—88 must be played quite smoothly. If the hands perspire, powder the hollow between thumb and forefinger up to first joint of the latter. Alum will do.

A good chin-rest is an indispensable adjunct to sure shifting, but only one which fits and grips the individual jaw will be found really comfortable or useful. It should be chosen personally and there is plenty of variety to select from. But the old-fashioned velvet-covered bar should be avoided; it is usually an instrument of torture and a challenge to toothache. Thin, slight figures with sloping shoulders require in addition some kind of pad or rest underneath the instrument. These can be made at home or procured in combination with the chin-rest, and that known as the "Sirex" is one of the best of which I have had experience. All chin-rests require to be attached with care, and if they arch over the tail-piece, may require to be filed in order to avoid undue pressure.

LESSON III.

HOW does your violin look when you take it out to begin your practising? Does it look fresh and clean and fit, the cherished tool of a careful workman; or is it dulled with the dust of ages, soiled and frayed of string and clogged with ancient rosin? Don't believe that age and pedigree are necessarily inferred from dirt and defacement. Many of the most valuable old violins would not betray their age to the uninitiated except, perhaps, by some exquisitely knitted crack or a thinning of the varnish here and there at points of greatest contact. No, he or she who has been lucky enough to become possessed of a mellow-toned instrument, numbering any decades over fifty, will be advised to keep it scrupulously clean and to handle it with tenderness, remembering also that it is liable to be affected by a warm or moist climate, and in such circumstances keeping a particularly watchful eye on any old cracks which may be inclined to re-open, and on the close adhesion of the ribs to the front and back tables. The case, even when closed, should not be kept by an open window, but in a sheltered corner of a warmed room, and should be well lined, or else the instrument itself carefully wrapped up to exclude as much as possible of the outer air. Transition from outside frosty air to a crowded, over-heated room affects both strings and wood, and should be graduated and minimised in any way that the circumstances afford; but that must be left entirely to the discretion of the player. When returning the violin to its case after practising, not only dust but the moisture of hands and of the breathing should be removed; the bow hair should be relaxed and the stick wiped with an old silk rag. All this has, of course, been said many times before, but I hope that those to whom it appears superfluous will pardon its re-appearance for the sake of others who may not yet have received so many or so direct reminders.

Let us imagine, then, that we start our practising with clean, true strings and an instrument as " fit " as our care can make it.

Schradieck, Groups IV. and V., first engages our attention. The student who can repeat even the first two exercises of Group IV. without discomfort to himself, and with the effect of clearness and equality to his hearers, has made quite a long step onward in the conquest of technical difficulties. These exercises cannot be played without having acquired some experience in the management of the bow and an understanding of the relative proportions of pressure to weight together with wrist manipulation. No one with a really stiff wrist need ever hope to be a violinist. But there are varieties of stiff wrist which are solely due to misunderstanding of the principles of bowing. Now, the ideal of bowing is to have such control of means and medium that any part of the bow can be made to produce approximately the same quality and quantity of tone, independent of its natural weight or lightness, distance from or nearness to the guiding hand. The forearm and upper arm are too heavy and too remote to play any but a subordinate part in the controlling action, therefore the responsibility rests on the wrist and the fingers. The latter are really the prime movers, the *rôle* of the wrist being an exquisite and intelligent obedience to the slightest hint of the first finger and thumb. Each finger, in fact, plays an individual part in a co-operative government, and this is one of the first things which the thoughtful violinist must realise for himself. One does not actually " play from the wrist," as has often been averred—one plays from the fingers *with the assistance of the wrist.* I think this distinction needs emphasis, because there are many would-be players who keep the fingers and thumb rigid, or almost so, upon the stick, and then lament that they have stiff wrists! It follows that, in order to give the fingers free play, the wrist must be sufficiently lifted whilst playing at the nut to prevent its weight being a drag. Changes of stroke at the nut are effected mainly by a swift and delicate balancing of the first and fourth fingers on the stick, particularly changes on the fourth string. All this, of course, belongs by right to the early days of instruction in bowing, but, judging by the number of students suffering from the artificial kinds of stiff wrist, it would seem to have been imperfectly understood.

Schradiek's exercises on bowing had better be taken with first eight, then sixteen, then thirty-two notes in the slur if any difficulty is experienced with the greater number.

Kreutzer, No. 10, is a delightfully candid study. The difficulties positively reach out a helping hand with a cheery "Here we are! Up you go!" sort of manner that carries the student on like a friendly wind at his back. Bars 13 (last half) to 16 are played in the 6th position, including the first note of bar 16. Keep as many fingers as possible on the strings throughout. Bar 18-19 contains a somewhat similar passage in the 5th position, returning to the first on the open note A. The top G is taken by extension from the 4th position, holding the first finger down and being careful to stop the following D in tune.

No. 11 is not so easy. Fortunately, it is intended to be taken at a walking pace. It consists of a series of shifts, the alteration of position usually occurring on a repeated note, which is a help to students who have doubts of a tune. But as the little finger is frequently responsible for the first note of each shift, it follows that it must literally and figuratively rise to the occasion and act with a decision and boldness not natural to it under ordinary circumstances. It cannot be permitted to feel its way upwards, nor yet to trail downwards (which imparts a most melancholy, not to say lachrymose character to the study), but must hit the bull's eye every time;—hit it strongly too. Upward shifts on the same string follow the usual rule of always gliding on the finger you have used, not with that you are about to use; downward ones are facilitated by holding the fourth or third finger immediately over the lower finger which it is about to replace on the repeated note. Whatever nervousness you may feel, don't clutch the neck of your violin. It is fatal; particularly if the hands get hot, and one can actually hear the wood protesting shrilly in the fork of the thumb (where, by the way, it ought not to be!) The second string is indicated wherever the similarity in fingering between the first and fifth positions might cause uncertainty, as in the third group of the first bar, which might have been played on the E string. The first notes of the final arpeggio are taken on the D string, and the final harmonic must follow perfectly naturally and without effort. A fault frequently noticeable in young students is that of making a perceptible break, like a singer taking breath, between the last stopped note and a high harmonic, thereby quite spoiling the effect.

We will now turn to Léonard, No. 4. This study depends much for effect on daintiness and brightness of bowing. A very little of the middle portion of the bow should be used for each staccato triplet, accenting slightly the first of each group, and using for the individual notes a minute portion—barely enough to make the string speak. Observe the graceful effect of the alternative legato slurs as introduced in the second bar and subsequently. The first note of these should not be too sharply accented, rather allowed to decrease towards the second note as if the mark were written thus $\Longrightarrow$ instead of so $>$. Do not alter the fingering in bar 8, and be careful not to play C$\sharp$ in bar 12, and wherever the imperfect 5th (F$\sharp$ to C) occurs. For the convenience of those who do not read French I translate the direction at bar 17, which reads, " without raising the third finger." In bar 30 and the following, and wherever similar passages arise, the fingers stopping the thirds:—

must be shifted simultaneously, as in double stopping. It would be wasted effort for the majority of players to attempt to get the F♯ in tune in bar 32 without previously removing the fourth finger. In bar 38 the second finger can be so placed upon the D string as to be able to stop and release the note C without being lifted. But if it is found difficult or impossible to play the C in tune in this manner, let the second finger be raised for each note. This applies also to bars 53 and 57.

The little Air with Variations which follows covers in miniature almost all the varieties of effect obtainable by technical means which are to be found in the greatest Air Variés by Vieuxtemps, Rode or De Bériot, and is an excellent introduction to these. The theme should be rendered quite simply but with feeling, and the phrases delicately finished, particularly in such bars as 15—16 and 27—28. Bar 26 is marked rallentando, but I am sure from the spirit of the music that Léonard intended the following bar to return to the original tempo. The same applies to the repetition.

The first variation is to be played a little faster than the theme. It should flow along like a brook in June, neither vehement nor thin, and when you come to bar 9 make the melodic notes stand out by a gentle pressure and a barely perceptible dwelling on each, but not by a sharp accent. In variation 2 let the bow have its way. It will wish to dance a little, and let it, so long as it does not degenerate into jumping. The marked notes should be drawn ever so slightly longer than the rest; but exaggeration of this will be a more heinous fault than omission.

C

The next variation opens with a mixture of slurred staccato and legato bowing, with which the student is already acquainted ; it is only in the rapid alternation of these that he may find a little difficulty. Bars 1 and 3, for instance, are the exact reverse of each other in effect, and bar 2 an admixture of both. At bar 9 (the alternative bars only count as one) the student must take care to detach the thirds clearly, and without roughness. Bars 13-15 are somewhat the same in style as bar 2, and will be found equally difficult to execute nicely.

The arpeggios in the Coda are comparatively easy. Finger the third bar so :—

and be sure to recover the natural position subsequently. Differentiate between legato and staccato.

LESSON IV.

THERE is a valuable little exercise for strengthening the fingers given, I think, by Alard, in the first part of his " Violin School," which I reproduce here for the benefit of those who require it. Place the first finger on F natural on E string; the second on C on A string; the third on G on D string, and the fourth on D on G string. Alternate the first finger and open string in a slow shake, keeping the others firmly in place. Then replace the first finger, and alternate the second and open string. Proceed in the same manner with the third and fourth fingers in turn. This exercise has not only the merit of strengthening the joints and enabling the fingers to act more independently of each other, but also trains them to stand clear of neighbouring strings, and is an excellent preparation for quadruple double stopping. It should not be practised for long at a stretch at first if the fingers ache afterwards. It may be practised also as left-hand pizzicato, giving the bow-arm a rest.

Schradieck, Group 6, does not call for any special remark. Nos. 9, 10, and 11, are good specimens of the sort of work which is frequently met with in orchestral accompaniments to solos in cantatas and oratorios, particularly by the second violins, and although not presenting any noteworthy difficulties, is nevertheless not always well executed by those who are unfamiliar with the progressions. No. 4 of Group 7 contains some very awkward fingering, and possibilities of false tune if the student is not careful in the beginning. All these exercises, and indeed any in which the student finds

C 2

a difficulty, should be practised at first with fewer notes in the slur, but the correct number should always be accomplished in the end.

In playing arpeggios of all kinds, perfect smoothness and equality is desirable (unless there are direct indications to the reverse), and all movement of the bow from string to string—and this is continual in arpeggio playing —must be made by raising or lowering the fingers from the wrist without any jerking of the elbow. In three-octave arpeggio playing, which is accented in triplets, the left forefinger must accomplish its various shifts without interrupting the even flow of the music, or in any way permitting the fact to be evident that it has an occasional difficulty in locating the higher positions. If a listener can tell that an arpeggio is difficult, depend upon it you are not playing it well, even though you may have acquired considerable speed, and got the intervals in tune. It should *sound* perfectly easy and natural; but it will not *be* perfectly easy to play it just so without continual and steady practice.

Kreutzer, No. 12, is written in the key of A minor; and the broken chord of the keynote, occurring at bars 1, 11, 17, 21, 27 and 31, will probably prove more difficult to play in good tune than those in higher positions, particularly the stretch between the upper C natural and A. Bars 7—8, I have found from experience, are more apt to be played out of tune than bars 9—10; and bars 15—16, 19—20, and 25—26 are also a little awkward at the first trial. But there is only one sort of difficulty to be overcome throughout, that of pitching the notes correctly, and, provided his sense of tune is sufficiently acute, the student is not likely to err therein unless he takes it at too great speed at the start.

Kreutzer's thirteenth study is like sundry people with whom most of us have met—very simple seeming on the surface but inclining to make one " sit up " on further acquaintance. The opening bars are much in the style of our favourite exercise, Schradieck, No. 4, Group III. Who can play the latter nicely will have the less difficulty with the Kreutzer. All the same, bar 9 is, to say the least, inconvenient, particularly if you are just ambling along, expecting nothing startling. Bars 10 and 11 also call for repetition. At bar 15 we come again into tranquil waters—but more apparently than really. At bar 29 the bowing alters. In the final bars the top note may be found a little difficult to pitch, but the effort is excellent practice as it must be a clean shot.

The thirteenth study in the Peter's edition is one not occurring in Litolff, and from this out students using the former must remember that their studies will read one in advance as regards number—Peters 14 being Litolff 13, and so on. The interpolated study is long but not difficult, except to those who have not yet acquired good control of the bow. The speed should be increased gradually.

No. 14 sets several traps for the unwary, and, as a preliminary precaution, the student should not attempt to play it unless the music is in a good light, as many of the accidentals are in very minute type. Each shake should last for an exact quaver, and should consist of at least one trill and a turn, as in example :—

The E is frequently made natural in the turn of the trill; but the student must be careful to play E flat in all places which are not marked otherwise. The second finger is used for the permanent note almost throughout the first line, but the trilling finger is sometimes a tone, sometimes a semitone distant, and the player has not only to make sure that his shakes are in tune, but must beware that he plays the right notes. The advice may seem superfluous, but experience has proved otherwise; particularly in relation to bars 7, 18, and 20. Bars 13—17 remain in the fourth position, with extension.

No. 15 is also on the shake, and should be practised
first according to the first example given at the head ;
the two succeeding examples given in the old Litolff
edition are useless; the turn should consist of seven
even, or nearly even notes. Bar 34 is a little difficult
to pitch ; and in order to accustom the hand to it, practise three bars, Nos. 33 to 35, over and over at various
unconnected intervals during the day's practising ; this
study presents no other difficulty.

We turn now to the sixth of Léonard's Studies,
written in very slow time. It is an example—almost
unique in violin studies, though commonly met with in
organ or pianoforte compositions—of what is called in
harmony a pedal note or point. The note E is the
dominant of the key (A minor), and through the greater
part of the piece is treated, through repetition, as the
pedal, though in the last two lines the part is taken up
by the tonic itself.

The pedal is, literally, a bridge over which many
harmonies pass, and in this instance the melodic notes,
which suggest the harmonies, must be very clearly
brought out, while the reiterated notes are firmly and
distinctly separated. The style is strongly accentuated,
but not a hint of scratchiness must be allowed.

There is an alternative and very different manner of
playing this study mentioned in the footnote, viz., with
springing bow, detached, in the middle, and in rapid
tempo.

No. 7 is on arpeggio playing ; but as regards fingering
it must be considered as quadruple double stopping, the
notes being seized almost simultaneously instead of con-
secutively, as in the earlier mentioned style of arpeggio
playing. This, in itself, constitutes a difficulty ; and
bars 9, 12, 13, 15, 19, 22, 23, 25, 26, 31, and 38, will
most probably not be conquered without a tussle. But
there is no royal road to facility in fingering chords, and
the fingers can be made supple and strong only by
repeated action.

It is better to play it through at first in smooth

slurring; afterwards giving the up-bow a jerk—almost a playful blow—which will cause it to rebound on the descending group. Keep the elbow about medium height, so that no extreme movement may be necessary, and the wrist perfectly free. The fingers should not hamper the natural elasticity of the stick, but merely prevent it from turning from side to side, and enable it to make the first note, practically the bass note, of each arpeggio very slightly more prominent than those succeeding. Use the full surface of the hair about the middle of the bow.

Bars 27—30 contain a hint of *bariolage*, a device more frequently employed in older than in modern violin music. It consists in playing a series of notes in one position, but introducing open instead of stopped notes whenever possible. Perhaps the present example hardly deserves to be called such, but it is usually found disconcerting to the student's sense of balance to take the lower note upon the higher string, and he or she is warned not to let the appearance of the bar alter the effect and manner of the bowing. This is a very pleasing study when well played, and I can quite conceive of its becoming a favourite when the preliminary difficulties are overcome.

Léonard, No. 8, though lengthy, does not call for any special remark. All that occurs in the Introduction, Theme, and Variations has been dealt with before wherever explanation seemed necessary. The fingering at bars 19—20 may be found awkward (the A being taken as a harmonic, and the fourth finger afterwards drawn back to G). Bars 22—23 are apparently intended to be taken in the same manner, but the student is recommended to return to the first position after the first E, and finger as before. The fingering in the last variation is left more or less to the student's discretion, and the varying results obtained by the choice will acquaint him with the excellence of forethought. In determining the best fingering one has always to take into consideration other matters as important, or more so, than mere left-hand convenience. There is the bowing, which is very dependent on fingering for both facility and effect; and also the temperament of the music, which calls for the quality of one string rather than another, for volume or for agility, all directly bearing on and influencing a nice choice. The student must equally avoid the substitution of what appears easy for what is more desirable, and, on the other hand, of what is showy and demonstrative for what is simple and natural.

LESSON V.

THE eighth Group of Schradieck's exercises, being in the second position throughout, presents no fresh obstacle to the student and serves to familiarise him with the notes naturally covered, with the exception of a few extentions, by the fingers on each string. Group 9, a mingling of first and second positions and extensions —some of the latter by no means convenient—contains some troublesome bars, which, if one may say so, puzzle both ear and hand because of a certain indefiniteness alike in tonality and actual position. For instance, in the second exercise the fingering in the first bar, in conjunction with the notes, most tantalisingly suggests the second position, which does not really occur until the following bar. In exercise 3 the harmonic progressions in the last half are so peculiar that, even admitting that Schradieck *may* have intended to familiarise the student with out-of-the-way progressions, we will nevertheless have mercy on him and introduce a natural before the D in the third group of the second bar, thereby turning the chord into an ordinary diminished seventh, considerably more agreeable to the ear. Exercise 4 should be practised slowly, and even with the aid of the piano (to which I have as a rule a strong objection) if the tune is doubtful in the parts where extension merges into actual change of position. The same applies to No. 5. Exercise 8, though fortunately possessing no tonal difficulties, makes exacting demands on the fingers, especially in the last bar, during which the hand must cover E and C sharp, not letting the first finger slip. It may be as well to remind players that Schradieck does not mark accidentals when the notes affected occur at a different octave—viz., the D sharp and C natural in the second group of bar 1, exercise 3.

Kreutzer, No. 16 (Peters, 17) is still concerned with trills. In order to make sure that it is practised strictly in time it will be just as well for inexperienced students to count twelve quavers in the bar at first. The tempo is slow, the bowing, at the point, strongly accented, and detached. At bars 28 and 29 make sure that the lower note of the octaves D and C, stopped with the fourth finger on the D string, is caught as firmly and clearly as the rest. With the opening third of bar 44 begins a passage which has brought tribulation to numberless players. Tune being the main difficulty, we cannot help them greatly, except to point out that the G flat is the only stationary note (not in fingering) and that in the double-stopping the E flat is two tones, the D flat one tone, and the C a semitone distant, respectively. Practise this passage very slowly.

Nos. 17 and 18, though useful studies, do not call for particular explanation. The fourth finger shakes may be found tiring, but must become strong and clear.

The examples, given at the head, of the various manners in which it is possible to play these studies cannot all be classed as trills, but though they be nameless, and in some cases irreducible to words, they will generally be found in practice to be good finger work. But there are too many studies on the same lines to be taken with advantage in the order in which they stand : both muscles and mind grow weary of such monotonous diet, and the practising relapses into drudgery, or, worse still, into slipshodness; so, after No. 18, we shall skip onward to No. 23 (Peters, 24) which offers us a variety of fare.

Octave playing is one of the severest tests of the amateur violinist, but it would be hard to meet with an exercise which introduces him more gently to a veritable " Pilgrim's Way " than this of Kreutzer's. The intervals are of a boldly melodic kind which support and fortify the sense of tune, and the repetition of each octave gives the beginner a second chance if he misses the first shot. It must be remembered that the stretch between the first and fourth fingers becomes less the higher up the neck we go; therefore, that in the simultaneous gliding from octave to octave the tone or semitone moved by the little finger will be a very little smaller than that moved by the lower. The left hand must be left quite free and the violin well supported at the shoulder. At the first time of playing, use more bow, legato style, and a moderately slow tempo; afterwards diminish the length of stroke and increase the tempo.

Léonard, No. 9, has really no technical difficulty; its only *raison d'être* is that one may acquire delicacy, elegance, and a more perfect control of crescendo and diminuendo; also that one may learn how to make the most of a contemplative, simple theme—a species of country landscape on a small scale—fertile fields and well-trimmed hedges alternating with here a young plantation, there a glimpse of ancient lawn sweeping about a mellowed home and hinting of old dials and clipt yew. Nothing tempestuous, nothing supreme, nothing passionate; only contentment, refinement, and a nice observance of bygone sweet courtesies. Very fanciful, you say? Well, no doubt; but flowing fancies blend themselves with music more kindly than stiff titles —and the "Moonlight" Sonata suggests many things more apposite than moonlight.

Etude No. 10, the Largo, is conceived in somewhat the same atmosphere, with the addition of a human interest. Two lovers wander through the sylvan scenes, embroidering, as lovers will, the recurrent theme, " I love you" with a thousand tender images; foreshadowing a little the minor moods of life, they finally unite— one soaring, one assenting,—in the fuller harmony of mutual faith. And if you would not disturb them, you must not let a trace of harshness or hoarseness mar the purity of your tones. Constrain every inch of bow-hair to yield you of its best—fulness, richness, mellowness; and let every tiniest note have just its value, neither more nor less. We recommend here, as once before, that the student should analyse and count (separating the beats into eight quavers) several bars silently before playing. Do not accent the beats; it spoils the continuity and spirit of the study; but *know* where every beat, and every half and quarter beats, falls. Analyse the time of bars 15 and 16 carefully. From bar 17-24 the character of the music becomes gradually more impassioned; permit yourself, then, a little licence in working up to bar 22, and broaden and slacken the last three quavers of bar 24 that you may recover the original tempo at bar 25. From this out the melody must be clearly sustained and the accompaniment dropped in delicately and lightly, but not drily. As regards fingering—the C in bar 31 is taken by considerable extension; do not let it go while playing the lower A. Take the passage from the half of bar 32 to the middle of 33 in the third position; then change to the second. In bar 35 take the A flat with the second finger and so slip into the third position for the succeeding notes. Pause on the final chord and let it fade into silence.

Léonard, No. 11, is more suggestive of an opening voluntary, the vicar somewhat late and the organist spinning his music wide and thin to cover the empty silence; nevertheless, it is a good and interesting study even if, from the artistic point of view, we might have had a little less of it. It is, of course, mainly wrist work, with a few passages that may require thinking out in the matter of fingering. At bar 28 adopt the second position, and continue therein till the latter half of bar 30. The *sforzandos*, frequently marked on the second page, will be found to have the effect—a quaint and charming one—of changing the rhythm every few bars. In such a very legato movement they should be pressed out rather than strongly accented. The broken-chord passages in the last three lines will test the student's skill in bowing: they should be perfectly smooth and of good volume except at the last two bars, which should be played diminuendo e rallentando. (The vicar is finding his place.)

LESSON VI.

THE tenth Group of Schradieck's exercises may be played through, but does not call for daily practising. Group 11 contains some useful exercises; notably Nos. 4, 5, 6, 7 and 11. It is now desirable that the student should alternate left-hand exercises with some devoted entirely to bowing. One way of acquiring volume and steadiness of tone is to see how slowly you can continue to draw the bow in one direction without letting the musical sound go off. The best way of measuring your power of doing this is to count slowly (at the rate of about 3—4 ticks of an ordinary small clock to a beat) up to 40 in each stroke, to begin with ; then increase the sum according to your increased facility. Better still, if you have a metronome, set it to 72 = ♩ each day and you will be able, by counting as before, to check your advance more accurately. The A string is the best on which to start all such bowing experiments. At the same time begin to practise the subjoined exercise in the following manner :—

Use the middle of the hair, keeping the forearm perfectly quiet (but not stiff) and letting the bow fall from the wrist so loosely that the fingers may swing it very slightly to and fro and off, taking a very tiny separate stroke for each note. Play *Moderato* at first and gradually work up to *Allegro*, when you will find

that, after the start, the springing motion continues
of itself if the muscles are not tightened. Do not be
disheartened if this style of bowing takes a long time to
acquire ; when once grasped it is never again lost,
and is a valuable asset to violinists, solo and orchestral.
In Kreutzer, No. 19, no more than a mordent can
conveniently be taken on each note marked *tr*. Counting the odd opening beat as a bar, we come, at bars
7—9, to some passages which are rather awkward to
pitch. Remain in the fourth and sixth positions,
respectively, for each full scale. Several similar
passages occur in the course of the study, but if the
first notes are pitched correctly the tune of the rest will
follow naturally.

No. 20 is played in the same way as regards the
trill, but is more tricky in rhythm as well as in fingering.
The study is played at the point of the bow and strongly
marked throughout, but the triplets must still be defined
even where the irregular trills appear to contradict the
regular marking. Alter the fingering in bars 15 and
32 (Litolff), taking the fourth note (F sharp) with first
finger in the fifth position.

When the student has practised the slow bowing
for a few mornings he might tackle the first study—
Adagio Sostenuto—which we have hitherto omitted. In
apportioning the stroke, reserve the greater length of
bow to produce the climax of the crescendo, and, for the
same reason, let it go a little more freely at the start
of the third bar ;—but beware of too great expenditure
or you may feel impelled to turn the final crotchets into
quavers. In fact, a tendency to curtail the time if
the stroke is running out is one of the chief things that
younger students will have to guard against throughout.
The glide from C to its octave at bars 33—34 may
require to be several times repeated before it is quite
successful, and the high F taken on D string in bar 69 is
also a difficult note to pitch. At bars 62—3 hold down
the G sharp and extend the little finger to the B. Allow
no perceptible break between the 64th and 65th bars,

and wherever a similar interval occurs; let the finger stopping the lower string glide delicately upwards on it to the position required for the higher note on the upper string. This applies particularly to bars 73 and 77, which are the more difficult on account of the crisis of the crescendo arriving simultaneously with the skip.

Do not be misled into playing the runs out of time because they are printed in small type; they are not really rapid. Two long and fatiguing shakes between the third and fourth fingers occur in bars 96—8 and 104—6. They could, of course, be taken with easier fingering, but it is worth while to attempt the harder before giving in. The letters *tr.* have been omitted in the 109th bar in some copies. The 25th Study in Peters is another excellent octave study which does not occur at all in the Litolff Edition. Students will now have to reckon identical studies *two* numbers ahead in Peters,— 24 Litolff being 26 Peters, etc.

We shall now proceed to No. 24. Probably one of the first things which the violinist will discover in this study is that he has an unexpected difficulty in stopping the E flat in the fourth position in tune in bars 3, 20, 42, and similar passages; the A flat in bars 25 and 43, and the G flat (sixth position) in bar 32. In the majority of cases the hand has got, so to speak, the set of the natural positions and has to become acclimatised to the alteration effected by the flat key. Remain, in each case, in the last position until a change is clearly notified by fingering. Bar 4, for instance, and the first note of bar 5 continue in the sixth position, and the latter half of bar 8 in the seventh. Bars 33—36 contain examples of the extension of a major tenth, and bar 37 of a minor tenth. By far the most difficult ones to stretch will be the B to D sharp in bar 36 and the B flat to D in bar 38, both being from the first position. It will be advisable to practise the bars containing them at the hour usually devoted to Schradieck ; but beware of over-straining the muscles. Bars 34—35 also may require repetition apart from the context in order to make sure of the tune. There is nothing new in the way of bowing; do not omit to play the odd staccato note following the slur.

Léonard, No. 12, is played at tbe heel, swinging the bow lightly from note to note with the fingers, the wrist being kept well up and very flexible. This study means work from first to last, and the passage from 17—30, which must be practised in sections, sets one as it were in mid-stream at once. Move all three fingers simultaneously. Repeat the first three couplets (of two quavers) until they are tolerably certain before you add the next three; then repeat the entire passage up to bar 24 before you go on to bar 25. Take the first couplet in bar 28 on the fourth, third, and second strings, but the last one in bar 29 with first, fourth and second fingers on the third, second, and first strings. Finger bar 47 in the second position; also bars 52 and 53. Put second finger on the B sharp in bar 72 and look to the tune. In the passage beginning at bar 84, and in the subsequent repetitions of it, the ascending scale is taken on A string the note E being played open throughout. From bar 95 —98 stop each successive sixth with the second and first fingers on A and D strings still using the open string for E. The passage beginning at bar 104, though very similar to that at bar 17, introduces some new combinations of fingering. Bars 115—119 will need to be practised in couplets very carefully before taking the passage through in the ordinary course. I should not advise the student to leave this study until he or she can play it with tolerable accuracy and ease, even though it may take longer than the preceding ones to master.

Léonard, No. 13, must not be attempted until some progress has been made with the *leggiero* bowing suggested for daily practice at the beginning of this chapter. Bars 5, 9 and 13, will probably need consider-able repetition before the player learns to subdue the tendency of the bow to jump wide. In bars 17—21 keep down the third finger, and from bar 23, the fourth, as there is no other aid to position or tune. Bar 29 starts a similar passage. Practise from 17—35, and all subsequent difficult parts, with legato bowing at first and very slowly, as the tune will not be easily maintained. The same sort of difficulty occurs between bars 66 and 83. At bar 124 we meet with a slight variation in the bowing; two notes are taken in the same direction instead of one; but the effect is obtained in the same manner as previously. The student is particularly warned against keeping his bow-hair screwed up too tightly. It should always be sufficiently loose to admit of a free curvative of the stick. Possibly, also, he is unaware that the hair tightens of itself in a dry atmosphere and slackens in a damp one. A sudden change of weather may cause a surprising and disconcerting variation in this matter, so it is as well to be prepared.

It would not be a bad plan to master the first half-page of this study before touching the rest—of course, committing it to memory—as it is much more useful to acquire a certain style satisfactorily than to play through a greater number of notes or even to attack ever fresh and increasing difficulties before one has really digested the previous ones. But all such remarks are only offered as suggestions. In the absence of personal knowledge it cannot be otherwise. The student must himself judge whether he is behind, level with, or ahead of the general scheme of work, and only use such portions of it as appear applicable.

No chance of duet, trio or quartet playing should be allowed to slip. There is nothing more educative as well as more interesting than associated playing undertaken in the proper spirit:—that is, with the intention to do the very best on all sides and not to be content with an inaccurate or colourless performance.

Remember that every composition worth playing must embody a definite mood, sentiment, or emotional idea, and you cannot be said to have done it justice unless you have conveyed this meaning to your audience or shared it with other performers. A colourless rendering

D

bears the same relation to true music as photography does to painting; endeavour, then, to be an artist; and keep discreet remembrance of your technical faults and shortcomings.

LESSON VII.

GROUPS 12 and 14 by Schradieck are mental rather than finger exercises. The 14th, in the fifth position, will be found easier than No. 12, both as regards the more or less mechanical pitch of the hand and the memorising of fingering, which is identical up to a certain point with that one string higher in the first position. No comment is necessary in either case, as it is for the student to familiarise himself with each; but it will hardly be necessary to repeat every exercise on the page as hitherto, but will be more profitable to pick out two or three of those best suited to his requirements from each group. All the same, an exception may be made in Group 13, in which every exercise contains something fresh in fingering or in the sequence of melodic phrases, and will repay diligent study. Indeed, the student is advised not to be in a hurry here, but to perfect each as far as possible before leaving the group.

Kreutzer, No 21 (Peters 22), accented in groups of six notes, will be found a valuable aid to velocity and dexterity of fingering. The student is warned to be on the look out for false tune in the abrupt changes of key, particularly at bars 19-20 and 28-29; also to note carefully the accidentals in small print. Practise slowly at first to ensure accuracy, afterwards increasing the speed according to individual capacity and preferably by a metronome, but not to a greater speed than $126 = $ ♩.

No. 22 is of similar style to No. 1, which was analysed in our last lesson; but, owing to the latitude in barring in this study, it is almost impossible to indicate on paper exactly how it ought to be played. Although the number of groups are variable in each bar, there ought to be a certain rhythmical proportion between them; —that is to say, if certain groups are taken faster or slower than others, it should be done by forethought and not by chance, and the same sets of notes should be relatively altered each time of playing once the player has made up his mind what arrangement will best bring out the character of the bar. As a general (but by no means dogmatic) rule the two or three first and last notes of each ornamental passage are taken a little more slowly than the central portion; but the bars in which passages shall be so dealt with must be left to individual judgment and taste, and there are some which, in their nature, indicate performance in quite even time. It is fairly safe to use a gradual crescendo in approaching the highest notes, and in bars 27 and 29, reserve the commencement of the decrescendo till the commencement of the descending scale. Bars 33 and 37 will need delicate handling : do not omit the rest in bar 37.

Marks of expression, particularly those relating to increase and decrease of tone, must not always be accepted without question as if they were the autograph of the composer. Sometimes, indeed, the composer is not so careful as he should be in regard to the accurate presentment of his meaning, and dashes them in as a general rather than literal indication of how the thing should be rendered. Or it may happen that the printer has taken liberties with the MS., and set them equal when they should be unequal, or not started or ended them on the exact note or notes that the character of the passage would seem to indicate. One must always obey the spirit rather than the letter in such things, and whenever these marks seem out of place, disregard or alter them. A questioning instinct is the parent of wisdom.

Kreutzer's 24th study (Peters 26), whilst not illustrating any particular species of technique, is, nevertheless, one frequently selected as an examination test, and, indeed, it somehow invites the casual player to be a little less than accurate. I don't know why this should be so, but it is. The intervals of major and minor tenths, taken by extension throughout, are not really so difficult to stretch except in the first position. In bars 3—5, continue in the sixth position until the first note of bar five, and finger corresponding passages similarly.

The twenty-fifth Study requires good, straight, firm bowing with a species of emphasis at the close of each stroke, which should not, nevertheless, be too abrupt or gruff. Bar 33 remains in the fourth position. In bar 39, slip the third finger from the note C to the D flat, and be careful of the tune in bars 43-44. There is a good deal of false fingering used throughout, but it is not a difficult study.

Léonard's 14th Etude promises employment for some time to come to those with weak or stiff fingers ; but as it is interestingly written and full of ingenious variety the practising of it will not be found so dry as if it were based more apparently on technical acquirements.

From the first to the sixteenth bar it flows along "sweetly and with elegance" and without the least inconvenience to the performer, but bars 7-8 would be more effective if the crescendo were to be prolonged up to the commencement of the shake in the eighth bar and diminished with the rallentando. (Do not shake more slowly, by the way, but dwell a little longer on each trill). With the modulation to the relative minor, in the seventeenth bar and onward, the music loses its restful character, and by the twenty-sixth bar we are in the thick of the struggle. Psychologically, it suggests a man who, with several irons in the fire, is straining to the uttermost to keep them all going, and dares not take an hour's rest for fear of complete disruption. It is quite a relief when, about bar 49, he begins again to get into smooth water and finally snaps his fingers at disaster.

The accompanying notes or chords must just be touched in clearly (but never harshly, though this is sometimes difficult to avoid on the second page) and not dwelt upon nor allowed to interfere with the even continuity of the shake. Play bars 24-26 in the fourth position. Take the accompanying semiquavers (beginning at bar 26) at the extremity of the down or up bows; then change stroke. The note B in bar 29 is taken by extension. Move into the third position on the third beat of bar 33, leaving it instantaneously for the first chord of bar 35: this last will probably require practice to effect neatly. From bar 37 onward the hand must cover the backward extension without losing grip. Bar 44 is best started in the second position, and, with the return to the major key, the sweet and tranquil character of the first part should be resumed regardless of the additional difficulties. In bars 57 and 58, pluck the *pizzicato* fifth with the little finger of the left hand—if you can!

In such affairs as expression and style, though one may prescribe the exact degree, place, and position in bowing and fingering by which it is most convenient to produce a given effect, one is none the less very far off from having really given the key of the matter to that number of students who are obliged to study by themselves. It is almost like trying to convey a sense of colour to one who has been born blind. Words, in such a relation, are but husks; one must first see and hear before the underlying spirit is manifest. And it is hearing—of the right sort—which is sometimes very difficult to come by, for those whose lines lie permanently in veritable "Sleepy Hollows." Once in a way, of a winter's night, they journey to a busier centre and listen with devout attention to a "star" player; returning in the small hours of the morning full of ideals and inspirations as to what may possibly be done in those solitary hours of practising. But weeks, perhaps months, pass before they hear anyone play again, and though the recollection of sweet sound is keen, the memory of details—of how such and such an effect was gained—becomes gradually fainter and less to be depended on. Then arises the danger of exaggeration, of rough and unskilful imitation, of degeneration. If such a condition, or indeed one of general discouragement comes about with you, it is better to go out into the fields and lanes and listen to the thrush's evensong, or the exquisite prelude of the nightingale, and become steeped in their sweetness . . . and forget all else.

LESSON VIII.

BY the time you have had your summer holiday, when the evenings close in, the fields and gardens are soberly pruned and clipt and already putting on their winter livery, you begin (I hope) to feel the stirring of desire for work—struggle—achievement. It comes with the first frosts, perhaps, a certain pleasant sharpness of energy, driving one up the higher scales like hills in holiday time, and topping the crest of difficulties as, not long since, we topped the crested waves.

Well, here's the programme for the present.

The amount and quality of exercises, such as Schradieck's, may henceforth be left to private judgment. Everybody learns in time what best suits his individual needs, and if he is wise will use just sufficient purely technical work to get his fingers into good working order and no more. Scales and arpeggios must, of course, be taken in moderate but regular courses: one can never afford to drop them, but too prolonged practising of them dulls the edge of interest. The last is a word for conscientious students, not for the triflers, who will probably be most eager to appropriate it.

Kreutzer, No. 26 (Peters 28) is singularly suitable to the season. It is decisive, clear, forceful; to be played in strict time and with scrupulous attention to legato and staccato phrasing; all demisemiquaver passages to be distinct and not too feathery. If you are out of practice, beware of bar 8. Bar 9 affords opportunity for a show of brilliance. In bars 21, 23, 25, 26, and subsequent similar passages, glide on the fourth string until your hand covers the high note on the first, and be careful to balance the bow neatly. Bar 24 will probably need some repetition, as may also the passage with extensions from bar 30 to 33, and bars 53 and 54. The study of No. 27 might be commenced in conjunction with No. 26, as being so distinct in style it forms a useful mental and technical contrast. Bars 5—6 might be picked out for preliminary practice; they form a key to the rest of the composition, and are a useful little bit of finger-work. The tune should be watched carefully throughout for fear the frequent use of extensions should, as it were, upset the balance of the hand, particularly if the student has not been practising lately. The bowing should be smooth and steady and the tone soft and clear, but not vague; this vagueness or veiledness is sometimes the result of too soft and uneven left-hand work—notes here and there which may be a little inconvenient to catch are insufficiently stopped, etc.

No. 28 is a roaring, blustering fellow, peering into every corner to see that there are no covered weaknesses and discrepancies, no languishing of tone or sentimentalities of tempo. From his entry, *staccato fortissimo* at the point of the bow, to the final semibreves, he gives the student but two brief breathing-spaces (the minims). He hunts vigorously, with a fresh broom, for mental cobwebs, and repeats his challenge (the opening bar) at every conceivable pitch and position.

Hold down the fingers firmly on the upper strings and watch the tune of the extension in such bars as Nos. 1 and 5. At bars 11 and 12 accent the sub-slurring and repeat bars 13-14 several times slowly:—indeed the whole study should be practised at a decidedly "walking-pace" at first. In the passage beginning at bar 19, consider your second finger (on the B flat) as a single anchor in a gale, and hold to it, playing from bar 28 in the same manner. The portion from bars 31 to 40 requires thoughtful practising, and a careful placing of the finger stopping the fifths; there is no interval

more liable to be played in false tune by a careless
or inexperienced player than a stopped fifth. Bars
45-48 will also require repetition apart from the context.
The remainder of the Study is chiefly recapitulation of
the earlier matter.

Léonard, No. 15, is marked *Allegro con fuoco* ; but there
is an old proverb very applicable here, which says, " You
must walk before you can run "—aye, and walk warily,
too.

One of the faults into which an inexperienced student
is often betrayed is, in the case of simultaneous sustained
melody and accompaniment, that of over-pressure on the
middle parts and weakness or inequality in the outer.
It is so difficult to apportion the balance of the bow
without much practice. But this Etude will afford
considerable assistance in the mastery of this particular
kind of playing. The first and third bars (which must,
of course, be fingered in third position with open string)
serve as a sample of the bulk, and should be played with
a steady even bowing, moderately loud, and without the
least harshness. The octave passages should be played
as far as possible on the same two strings. Look out
for false tune in bars 13 and 14, and take bar 15 as well
as 16 entirely on D and A strings. Bar 17 is taken
in second position. In the passage from bars 20 to 27,
be careful to sustain the dotted quaver, and keep a
steady and sweet tone throughout. Do not let the bow
be affected by the action of the left hand. Change
position for each chord without lifting the fingers.
Finger bars 29 and 30 in the fifth position and bar 31 in
the third and first positions. Bars 38 and 39 are
executed similarly to bar 40, though they look so much
more complicated. The fingers stopping the interval of
the tenth (first and second) are simply moved upward on
G and A strings till they reach the tenth position, the
open D being employed throughout. From bar 41 to 60
nothing particularly requiring comment occurs : the
interposition of a quaver rest facilitates rapid changing
of position. In the 69th bar change strings for the last

three octaves. The passage beginning at bar 76 is difficult to play nicely. The three strings must be caught practically simultaneously for the chords, but the upper string instantly quitted. It may not be found easy to do this and to sustain the two lower strings with an even bow and without involuntarily accenting the second semiquaver, but thoughtful practising will gradually lead to mastery. The first and third fingers (left-hand) should be employed here for the double-stopping throughout, except, of course, for the last third in bar 78. Do not omit to sustain the minims from bar 84 to 87. Bars 97 and 98 are taken in the fifth position, and bar 99 begins in the fourth. The octave passages starting at bar 106 are an excellent bit of practice, and should be adopted as an occasional exercise for odd moments. It is rather a good plan to note down all such bars as No. 106, or tricky short passages that will bear separation from the context, on a spare sheet of music paper, and, after a little time, you will have collected quite a useful and unique set of technical exercises—those, too, specially adapted to your individual needs, as you are not likely to take the trouble to note bars which have given you no check on your way.

If it should happen that you have no accompanist with whom to practise, even occasionally, your pieces, or an uneducated accompanist, which is worse than none, it will be found necessary, or at any rate very helpful, to make a study of the pianoforte parts as well as the violin. If you can play the piano even a little you will arrive at some idea of the composer's meaning as a whole; without such a conception it is useless to attempt the study of Sonatas or any similar compositions of serious intention. Apart from the loss in the artistic point of view, the distraction of mind inseparable from hearing the part of the second instrument for the first time is very apt to disqualify solitary students who enter for examinations without previous familiarity with the accompaniments to their pieces. But it is by no means necessary to be able to perform showily before you can attain to a practical acquaintance with your pianoforte parts; sound theoretical knowledge is the essential thing. Phrasing, on the piano, is very similar to bowing on the violin, or can be understood in much the same sense, and it must by no means be left out of consideration, as contrary accent and contrasted phrasing are frequently used to bring out the individualities of the instruments and to heighten the effect of certain moods or styles of music.

LESSON IX.

K REUTZER, No. 29 (Peters 31), like a nettle, must be grasped firmly or it will sting; in other words, it will continue to be imperfect and un-mastered if it is attacked with a light, hasty touch instead of a brilliant, decisive one. It looks simple; but, like a good many innocent-looking human beings, it will be found to have more in it than appears on the surface. Kreutzer delights in trills, which in this case are merely turns, or even mordents, and must be sharply accented with both bow and finger. Except for a little bit on the top of the second page it is practically a study in semitones, which is just as well to remember, as it explains why the fingers sometimes suffer from a sort of cramp after practising it. It should be played at first slowly, and afterwards, by degrees, worked up to a good pace.

In No. 30, we have a preliminary study in double stopping. It is a very easy one—chiefly scale passages over a stationary note—and will be found of considerable assistance to those who have a slight difficulty in deter-mining tune. A good many players find the tune of double stopping much more perplexing than that of single. They have a difficulty in deciding which note of two is false. Of course this implies an imperfect musical ear, but is so common a weakness amongst the average run of violinists, who play just for the pleasure they derive from their own efforts, that it is as well to accept it as a possibility and warn those who suffer from it not to fatigue the ear—and thereby increase the dullness—by prolonged repetition of the puzzling passage. Repeat only a few times, and return to it frequently after an interval of less trying work. I should recommend that No. 30 be taken with two bows per bar at first; but the student who has been playing Léonard is not, of course, new to the subject. All the same, he will find this a useful exercise.

No. 31 is a little more difficult, but by no means to be dreaded or shirked. The thirds which are taken with third and extended fourth fingers must be watched ; they occur frequently and may be found a little awkward at first trial. The passages from bars 21-27, and 27-34 should be practised separately; indeed the whole study had better be taken in sections at first, paying attention solely to tune, and afterwards with regard to bowing, phrasing, and other niceties of expression. In many cases the student will probably say to himself or herself : "Well, I know an easier, and I believe a better fingering for such and such a passage." It is quite true that a simpler fingering might be adopted with quite as satis-factory results, *for the time being*; but the majority of studies are written with the object of giving the learner knowledge of, and exercise in, fingerings and technical details with which he might otherwise remain un-acquainted, but which, nevertheless, are necessary for æsthetic reasons in the higher walks of violin playing.

We will now turn to Léonard, No. 16 ; that is, those to whom double stopping presents no special and peculiar difficulties will do so ; but if this individual difficulty be strongly felt, certain students will do well to postpone work on this study till they have greater mastery of the subject, and to practise No. 17 instead, in conjunction with Kreutzer.

The opening Adagio, and its repetition with variations at the close, contains a good deal over and above the ordinary difficulties of fingering to test the musical qualities of the student. First of all there is the tone, which must be sustained, even and round; secondly there is the manner, which is dignified ; and the details of expression, which are barely hinted at and left to be filled in by the executant. We will draw attention to points of possible error or weakness bar by bar as they occur. The last note of the second bar, for instance, may be out of tune, also the first and widest tenth in the third bar. Begin the fifth bar in the second position with extension for the note F♯ (as in Kreutzer, No. 31). In the seventh bar do not let the tone on the sustained G go whilst changing the finger; take the F♯ by backward extension. The fifth (D and A) in the next bar is taken with two fingers instead of, as usual, one; beware that they stop truly and stand well clear of each other. Bar 14 lends itself to false intonation, and the downward glide must not be coarsely executed. The Risoluto portion in the relative minor, is, as the word implies, of a contrasted character. The dotted crotchets must be sustained for their full value, and the succeeding semi-demisemiquavers played very distinctly and *in tune;* speed is not a valid excuse for impure tonality, and these groups had better be practised slowly and repeatedly at first, as several of them are by no means easy. As the three final chords in each bar are played throughout with down strokes, an unpleasant chippiness of tone must be carefully avoided, and the two top strings must be sustained for the brief value of each chord—the general tendency will be to make them too brief and dry. At bar 26 return to first position for the chords, but at bar 28 take the first chord in the fifth and other two in the fourth position. Extend the fingers well for bar 29. In bar 35 take the last D of the broken-chord group on open string, it will thereby be easier to get the high octave. At bar 39 we return to the original Tempo and manner, but with additions and variations. The student has been told elsewhere how best to treat a sustained melody with accompaniment, so it will not be necessary to go into the matter again. The last bar but one needs execution at once delicate and sure in order to be effective.

No. 17, from the technical point of view, is concerned chiefly with bowing; and a very charming and graceful

study it is. The first five quavers of every second bar
should be repeated till the pitch of the top note is
attained without hesitation before going on to the rest.
About a third of the down stroke near the point should
be used to start the bar, and the succeeding stroke
should be less than half spent before the *sf.* chord is
reached. If the bow runs too far and too swiftly it is
apt to get beyond control, also, it will be more difficult to
get into position for the next short down stroke. The
portion of bow used for each staccato semiquaver must
be very minute, and directed from the right first finger.
The fingering is comparatively straightforward all
through. Observe the legato slur within the up stroke
which begins to occur from bar 35. Adopt fingerings
throughout this portion which will admit of the four
strings being crossed by the bow whenever possible.
Play the final staccato passage pianissimo, and with the
utmost delicacy.

The course laid down for this study is so varied
both from the technical and from the artistic points
of view that it ought to afford considerable interest to
very different sorts and grades of students. Those
who can play these studies with accuracy and spirit may
rest assured that they are making good progress ; but
mere speed, or a rough-and-ready style of performance,
must not be taken for any measure of perfection. A
good test of that progress—which, no doubt, most of you
have already tried—is the playing over of back studies
which had been found especially difficult when first
attempted. If the difficulties are difficulties still, to any
great or noticeable extent, there is a breakdown or
omission somewhere in your scheme of work. Be content to go back and try to pick up the broken thread.
Find a study, if possible, which is written to illustrate
your particular weakness, and attack it with determination. The very meeting with the thing in a fresh
dress may lay the ghost which, perhaps, was only a bogie
raised by nervousness. If your fingers hear an inward
voice crying, " This is the thing I can't do ! " as soon as

it comes in sight, they will balk, like a horse at a fence when his rider is doubtful. But if you persist in saying "What is the best way to conquer this thing?" they will soon come to your assistance with a subconscious wit of their own.

LESSON X.

HOW many of you, invisible readers, are fond of getting up early ?—or if fond is an extreme word, how many of you can with reasonable cheerfulness anticipate the wintry dawn for a good purpose ? I am moved to this question by the case of A., whose spirit has suffered eclipse for lack of variety. A. goes to work at 9 a.m., returns about 6.45, and at 7.30 starts practising. He continues till 10 p.m., or as much later as landlady and fellow-lodgers can be induced to tolerate. Having kept this up for about eighteen months, with only a brief break, he feels discouraged and dissatisfied. Even the conquest of a bristling difficulty no longer gives him the joy he felt in times past. Why ?

Because he has run his hobby to death. If A. were to take one hour's practising in the morning, even with a mute—which I don't countenance except in the face of domestic exigencies—and to keep one hour, or more, in the evening for walking, reading, or even the study of another subject, and at the same time to avoid practising in a groove, he would find his zest for fiddle-playing gradually returning.

It matters very little what we can do unless we take an interest in doing it, and in the case of a hobby it is pure lunacy to pursue it to boredom.

Kreutzer, No. 32 (Peters 34), is a precise and careful fellow, taking us over and over the same ground lest by any chance there should be an unsound note in us within the limits of his special duty, and indeed, by the time he has done with us, we ought, at any rate, to be able to play the common chord and chromatic ninth in D major in our sleep. It is of the nature of Schradieck, this study, and equally useful for the fingers; not likely to give a conscientious student any trouble, but containing a few bars here and there—Nos. 6-7 and 37-8, for instance—which might trip the unwary player, and which if not stopped exactly in tune, are better not played at all, as they would merely encourage a habit of careless intonation. Bar 27 flaunts a red flag for those whose sense of pitch is not well developed, also bars 25-26, 47 and 50.

The succeeding study, the *Marche* in E flat major, is a capital specimen of violin music of the Handelian style—broad, flowing, and of well-marked tonality. Those who still keep a corner of their hearts for the Handel violin sonatas will seize upon it joyfully, and, let us hope, with no humming and hawing, and groping for the opening chords. Take up your bow with purpose, and start like the sun breaking through a cloud. Of course you may start wrong; nothing more likely in a good many cases. But it won't be a bit more wrong for having struck with confidence, than if you tip-toed up and felt your way about it as if it were a piece of green bog-land. The right spirit is greater than literal accuracy by the span of a sea to a lake.

Confidence is the key-note of this study. It deals with no trickeries either of left hand or right, but demands of us full voice, breadth, and a mellow geniality. Beware that you have a true understanding of the phrasing starting at bar 17: the tone broadens on the dotted quaver, and it must not be curtailed to favour the staccato semiquaver which, as it were, pounces playfully upon the succeeding chord. In the twenty-fifth bar try to enlarge the G♭ without disturbing the sustained minim. In bar 27 alter the bowing in the latter half so as to bring the twenty-eighth bar on an up-stroke, and sustain the tone. The latter half of bar 94 will probably need considerable repetition before it comes off quite naturally; but, on the whole, all goes with a clear sky and a favouring wind.

The bowing of No. 34, in E minor, is accented with somewhat the effect of a lame step, and the fingering conspires to heighten the impression, notably at such places as bars 7-8, 55-58, and 63-5, but there is no mental difficulty which may be cleared by comment, and ordinary care and practice are all that is required. All the same, it will be wiser to take it in small portions at the start, though the first ten bars really contain the gist of the whole thing.

Léonard's eighteenth Étude will be found a pleasing contrast to the above. There is a certain similarity in technical detail, as regards bringing out the melodic notes by carefully regulated pressure of small portions of bow-hair, but the result to be obtained is entirely different. In this there must be no jerking. Though the melody must stand out, it must be without sharpness; rather, as it were, with bevelled edges, and an evenness of flow and volume. It will be more difficult to attain to this, with any degree of perfection, than to achieve the Kreutzer study; moreover, the student must understand the phrasing before it becomes possible. For instance, the first six melodic notes constitute the first phrase, the following two, on G string, are merely an echo, and must be kept subordinate in the matter of volume and emphasis. If there is any doubt in the performer's mind as to the limit and intention of these phrases, it will be well to play over the melody *alone* first, that he may feel where the cadences lie, and which notes are merely echoes and not an intrinsic part of the phrase. Of course a knowledge of elementary composition would at once set such questions at rest, but, failing this, the student must trust to his musical feeling. The notes *look* alike throughout, but to play them so would imply an utter misunderstanding of the meaning of the piece, and would result in most melancholy monotony.

The nineteenth Étude, also, is mainly a matter of bowing, though of a different kind. Those students who have not already made a study of this particular kind of bowing are advised to do so (using the chord of G major as a basis) in the "Schradieck" hour for a few days in advance of starting the actual piece. Probably this advice is unnecessary. Let us hope so, as this bowing, though most effective in achievement, is not at all easily acquired by some students. As in learning to ride a bicycle you were, no doubt, told not to look at the wheel, so, in practising springing arpeggios, you must have ceased to think of the bow before it really moves happily. For this reason it is not well to begin to learn the bowing on the study. Get the trick first ; use it afterwards.

LESSON XI.

K REUTZER No. 35, in F minor (Peters 37) offers no especial difficulties, except, perhaps, in bowing. It requires swift, decisive action from right wrist and forearm in order that the alternate strokes may start from point or nut as directed; particularly if it is played really *Allegro vivace ;* but *Allegro moderato* will be more likely to suit the majority of students. Beware of false intonation from bars 24—26, 29—30, and from 38 onwards.

The succeeding study, *Allegro Moderato* in D major, though not very attractive as a composition, is nevertheless interesting because of the kind of violin-playing which it illustrates. Much of the older violin music— certain movements for instance of the Bach solo sonatas —is written in two-part, sometimes in three-part style, one which, while it presents to the performer few conspicuous difficulties, nor indeed seems to the un- initiated listener to exhibit any profound technical skill, is in reality a very high test both of intelligence and dexterity on the part of the violinist. In practising this study the student must carefully differentiate between sustained parts and notes which are merely touched in, and according as he becomes familiar with the pro- gressions, must introduce variety in volume of tone and neatly round off the phrases. For instance, the first three bars might each be played so ⋖ ⋗ with the crisis on the third beat, and the fourth bar phrased with a repeated diminuendo ⋗ ⋗ . This, of course, is merely put forward as a suggestion, and several other ways of rendering it might be just as effective; but the main point is, that there must be some rhythmical plan intelligently conceived and carried out, else the thing remains a mere jumble of notes. As regards fingering :—move into the second position on the last group of the second bar; use the fingering indicated for second and third groups in bar fourteen with change of position for the two similar succeeding groups; in the 26th bar the sustained minim must be changed from stopped to open string with delicacy; the last group of bar 28, and first of 29 also requires dexterous use of the fourth finger; and the same applies to the following passages. Sustain the semibreve throughout in bars 54 and 55, and be careful of the intonation in the last two groups in bar 62. If properly rendered the whole study should flow with the utmost clearness, smoothness and ease.

No. 37, in A minor, contains more musical variety and will, no doubt, appeal more widely to the average player. One must take for granted that each one has at least a little knowledge of phrasing and melodic construction —otherwise he will be apt to play the fool with this and similar studies where the bowing alone does not indicate the design. As regards other warnings and hints :— analyse the time in bar 15, and in bar 43 take the bow lightly off the first staccato quaver and leap to the point for the legato phrase (in which the fourth finger is used in extension). Hold the sustained notes for exact duration from bars 49—54. Bars 66—68 may require repetition, also the passages in fourth position starting at bar 135.

No. 38 is, of course, entirely concerned with shakes, and as regards this, the manner of playing depends very much on the pupil's facility in trilling. In any case, whether a rapid, or comparatively slow trill is adopted, the change from note to note must be made with as little break as possible. They are all single shakes, may be practised with or without turns, or with only occasional turns as the phrasing warrants, and taken on the upper or lower notes according as marked. The fingering is determined by the position of the trill.

Léonard's 20th Study is well described by its title
—*Duetto*. It is by no means an easy piece of music.
At the 31st bar it introduces a variety of tremolo that
promises trouble to those not very devout practisers.
In that very bar it will be necessary to alter the fingering
to the half position in order to sustain the quaver E
sharp, returning to the ordinary for the succeeding
quavers. That change is a key to the fingering throughout—a series of alterations, often on identical notes
in one part.

Observe the strong contrasts of volume and quality of
tone. In spite of the extreme softness of the tremolo,
produce a clear, sweet tone in the melodic notes, not
veiled.

This study affords a good introduction to the central
part of the slow movement in Mendelssohn's Violin
Concerto—a part which deters many violinists from
attempting an otherwise attractive and playable solo.

No 21 may either prove a mere bagatelle or exactly
the reverse, according to the amount and kind of training
the student has bestowed upon his right forearm, wrist
and fingers. Everything depends upon being able to
utilize, under control, the natural elasticity of the stick.
It is not possible, even in a moderate tempo, to *make*
separately each tiny stroke. What you have got to do is
to set the bow going with just the right amount and kind
of spring and then let the notes, as it were, happen of
their own accord. This advice will be Greek to some
and A B C to others. To those to whom it presents
little comfort I say, "Hope on." Though you labour at
it exceedingly, with pain and grief, at the eleventh hour
the trick will come, suddenly, and you will not lose it
again. Hold the bow very flexibly; let the third finger
prevent excessive springing, and see to it that the
first joint of the first finger and the thumb are thoroughly
supple. Finger the third and fourth bars in the third
position ; the fifth and sixth bars in fifth position, and
follow the same system throughout, using false fingering
whenever desirable.

The 22nd Study deals with yet another species of tremolo used as accompaniment to a sustained melody. Similar styles of violin-playing have so frequently been treated of in these papers that it will be unnecessary, now, to do more than remind students to keep the accompaniment well subordinated to the melody. This may seem a short lesson as regards printed directions, but the studies will probably take longer to master in style than in bulk. The student who has followed so far with any degree of real facility or honest mastery has left the days of mere groping a long way behind. But the question of the actual worth of his progress is not one, unfortunately, that he can, himself, answer. It must be referred to a competent teacher. An incompetent one, however apparently successful, should he have the ill luck to trust to unreliable report in this, to him, serious matter of lessons, will either tell him that he is a budding genius, or try to cure his almost inevitable faults and misapprehensions by a species of musical quackery. In either case he will be irretrievably spoilt.

But if a violinist feels that he has genuinely gained some insight into playing, no matter how backward he may feel himself to be in regard to special branches of technique—*staccato* bowings and the like—it is worth his while, now, even at some sacrifice, to obtain the personal direction he requires. But let him first make very careful inquiry as to the style of pupils the selected professor turns out before closing his bargain. The further one is from an active educational centre the more difficult it is to obtain good lessons in anything, and the more gaily and fearlessly the uncertificated man brings up his flock in ways they should not go. He is safe in the remoteness of competent criticism. But do not lose hope. Even the best teachers visit districts very widely afield nowadays, although, perhaps, at somewhat longer intervals than those closer at hand, and a little certain light may illuminate large tracts at present sadly dim.

LESSON XII.

IN Léonard No. 23 we have a very different affair from the last, plenty of variety, interest, and above all, of exercise for slack or stiff left hands. For the *staccato élastique*, dash the bow on, near the point, with just sufficient force to enable it to take the remaining notes in a series of rebounds. If the left fingers at the same time stop with hard brilliant touch it will materially aid the effect. Those runs apparently starting with a shift should really be taken with the hand already in the position desired and the first finger extended backward for the opening note. The double-stopped thirds and sixths may be taken by shifting the same couple of fingers a semitone. At bar 13 first occurs a peculiar-looking passage, but it is really only a repetition of the kind of bowing to which we were already introduced in No. 21 ; both notes must, of course, be held down. From bar 17 and onwards, make the left fingers fall hard and clearly, and observe the accented notes. The arpeggios starting at bar 31 will need careful handling in order to render them, there and elsewhere, with due distinctness and yet with delicacy. Keep the three strings going in bars 66 and 67, and two from bar 68 out. The final pizzicato is, of course, left hand.

The 24th and last Etude, the so-called " Prelude," comes rather like a trickle of cold water after the others. We have become so accustomed to pleasantnesses here that this—" Bah ! " says the disgusted student, " No music here, anyhow ! "

Well, it is rather dry, quite exceptionally dry if you like, and not in the least resembling Léonard's usual style. None the less, it would be unwise to skip it.

There is no other precisely similar in the course; yet good scale work, particularly with modulations, is a very essential branch of violin playing. Accuracy, smoothness, and evenness of volume, are the qualities necessary to the right performance of this ugly duckling, which, in spirit and in the future, may yet prove swanlike.

Kreutzer, No. 39, in F major (Peters 41), is much the most difficult piece of work we have as yet attempted. It has, like an earlier study, some surface points of resemblance to a Bach Chaconne. The difficulties it presents are mainly mental, but it presupposes well-trained fingers. Throughout the study it is necessary to have strict regard to which notes are intended to be sustained and which are only to be lightly touched in; also to the somewhat unusual fingering chosen to this end. The double shakes should be picked out and practised separately. Bar 15 is a sample of a difficult progression: lean on the first beat, but be sure not to miss the bass of the second, softer chord. Almost every bar contains something that will give the student occasion for pause and thought, but they are not difficulties which can be materially lightened by advice on paper. One can only recommend to the tolerably efficient student patience and perseverance, and to him who feels that it is as yet outside his capacity, total omission in preference to imperfect mastery.

The last study is within the reach of all. It is bright, tuneful, and contains no pitfalls. There are several pretty and ingenious turns of phrasing compassed by various bowings. Let me remind fiddlers that sustained notes on a violin are not always sustained in the exact manner of a piano or organ, particularly in two—or three-part harmony. They are treated sometimes with alteration of fingering, sometimes transferred to other strings, or, as at the start of bar 70, it is sometimes impossible to avoid actual re-striking. But this last must always be done with as little indication of the change as the performer can achieve. In this same passage (from bar 70) the phrasing on the second string can certainly be brought out without interrupting the long notes.

With this we bring our Scheme of Study to a close. No one knows better than the writer how many apprehensions and uncertainties may have arisen over such general directions and suggestions as it has alone been possible to give ; but it remains to hope that it may have been of some use to those students who are desirous of making a measurable progress in view of what the future may bring of more favourable opportunities. To them I would speak a little more fully of the uses of recapitulation.

We may presume that some months have elapsed since each student started the Course, and even granting that the practising did not amount to more than one hour per day, it ought to make an easily appreciable difference in the performance of each individual. There is no surer way of finding it out than by going back to the beginning, going over the old ground and inspecting the old pitfalls. Are they pitfalls still ? How do you stand, now, regarding intonation ? Can you finger with more assurance in the higher positions ? Do you understand why certain passages are fingered in one way and not another ? Can you render rapid cross-string passages without getting into trouble with the bow ? Have you acquired greater control of the bow with reference to gradation of tone as well as evenness and delicacy ? Has your capacity for producing volume of sound increased ? Lastly, has your musical intelligence kept pace with your technical development ?

Now, it is probable that you cannot answer sundry of these questions—particularly the last—to your own satisfaction, or, indeed, to the satisfaction of a teacher; but of others you will be able to form a very fair estimate by repeating the two books of studies before passing on to a fresh course. It will not be necessary to play every one ; not all the trilling studies in Kreutzer, for instance ; but each that is representative of a special idea, or which caused you previous delay in mastery.

Whatever writer's studies you take up next, it will be found an excellent plan to take at the same time a course of Sonata study—Mozart or Schubert before Beethoven. Some of the modern Sonatas are extremely interesting, but, as a rule, they are more technically difficult than the classical and therefore less satisfactory to essay without aid. It will be very necessary, also, to seek a pianist. To play together once a fortnight, or even once a month, is better than not at all, if circumstances do not lend themselves to more frequent meetings. But the pianist must be in earnest as well as the violinist or the conjunction will lead to disaster. A proper respect for and mutual understanding of one another's respective rôles is essential between Sonata players, and any tendency to "show off" on either side must be nipped in the bud. Granted this understanding, there is no more enjoyable side to violin playing, with the exception of the string trio or quartet.

To conclude, I wish those students who have travelled with me so far a very real success in their efforts, which they would not have continued to make had they not been prophetic of at least a measure of victory. There is always something left to learn about the violin. No matter how industriously one may have climbed there is sure to be one hill more on the horizon when the sun goes down. But that, after all, is the charm of the voyage. Who wants to journey for ever on a plateau? Were it not for these hills to climb life would be very dull; and dullness is more insupportable than even the chance of disaster.

Occasional Papers on Violin Matters.

ON PLAYING AT SIGHT.

THERE is almost everything to be said in favour of the habit of playing without notes, but there is just a little to be adduced against it—the latter, hardly so much an objection to the act of memorising, as a caution not to abuse it to the suppression of other things of equal value.

It has been remarked that the good memorist is seldom a good sight-reader. I do not know why this should be so—unless the one faculty is unduly strengthened at the expense of others ; but the impression prevails, and there may be some truth at the bottom of it.

Nowadays, the tendency to specialise is so great that, even within the limits of the chosen subject, there is often a species of favouritism exercised in the details of technique, mental and physical. To make this plainer— the soloist concentrates all his powers upon the conception and interpretation of a comparatively small amount of music : the orchestral player devotes his entire energies to the breaking of new ground ; to rapidity of perception rather than a more enduring insight.

A certain bias in one direction or the other is inevitable, according to the gifts and capacities of the musician ; but the chief inclination need not be indulged in to the exclusion of the other. Both faculties—that of rapid perception as well as that of memorising—should be cultivated side by side in the early days of studentship.

The average child rather prefers to play from memory

F

(aural, not ocular) though the performance is often very faulty. Ask the same child to play at sight a simple piece, well within his powers, and he will probably turn upon you in pained surprise, because he has not been taught from the start that reading is an essential part of music-study.

It ought to be unnecessary to emphasise this; but I have had pupils sent to me, adult as well as children, who had no more idea of interpreting a page of new music than they had of navigating a balloon; yet they could sail through two or three tuneful pieces fairly correctly. What drudgery encompassed the learning of them, heaven only knows!

This kind of mental spoon-feeding is most wearying to both teacher and pupil, and unproductive of any permanent result. The pupil, however young, should realise from the beginning that the page before him is not an assortment of lines and dots, printed for his special penance, but the representation of some definite feeling or idea—joyful, tranquil, martial, or sad,—to be played, as nearly as he can, in the manner indicated by the title and tempo. Difficulties should be practised separately, not dwelt upon at the first performance, for fear they should obscure his view of the piece as a whole.

Never let him dissociate the signs from the spirit of music. It may cause a little more intellectual expenditure on the teacher's part to consolidate this connection during the earlier lessons, but the results are thoroughly worth the trouble.

No one who cannot seize the prevailing manner of a composition at sight—though he may fall short of technical excellence—can claim to be a thorough musician.

Quite a number of young teachers, after they have obtained their diplomas and started on their professional career, find it still necessary to be themselves taught certain pieces that they may in turn teach them to others. Of course every one understands that difficulties may arise at times in which the advice of an older and more experienced musician is desirable. It is the *practice* of "running up to town" for tuition in the pieces being taught—possibly chosen from an examination syllabus—which is reprehensible, as it argues a want of insight on the part of the younger teachers, and must impart an inelastic and formal quality to their methods of instruction. They lack the power of spontaneous interpretation, and seek to cover it by mere imitation, parrot-wise. This arrangement may even be moderately successful with a performer; but a teacher who lacks initiative can never hope to be otherwise than mediocre, or to inspire his or her pupils with that confidence which is the natural atmosphere of earnest effort.

F 2

BAD HABITS INCIDENTAL TO
CHILD-VIOLINISTS.

THEY are not nearly so bad or so numerous as those laboriously acquired by adult players; but they exist, nevertheless, and must be promptly checked. A few hints as to those most common may not be out of place.

A habit which is likely to have serious future consequences is that of slightly protruding the right hip whilst standing with the whole weight of the body thrown upon the left foot. This attitude of resting upon the left foot is technically correct; but if persisted in for too long at a stretch it is apt to permanently influence the form of a growing child, especially in the case of one that is slight or delicate.

Discretion may be exercised in the matter of rests and occasional changes of position, and in this the watchfulness of the parent or guardian must supplement that of the teacher.

The trick of leaning the left elbow and upper arm against the body of the performer is one that commends itself to almost every little beginner. The extended position is so unusual and fatiguing at first, and the neck of the violin nestles so snugly into the hollow between the first finger and thumb, that, doubtless, it is very grievous and discouraging to be sternly told that it is all wrong, and that the hand must be left loose and free to stop the notes, and by no means used as a mere prop.

Have we not all been through it—those of us who were not geniuses? And it is just as well that we should look back sometimes to long and weary half-hours of our own initiation, and let them teach us mercy towards the present generation of embryo fiddlers.

I have occasionally permitted pupils, whilst learning to draw the bow across the strings, to rest the head of the instrument upon the ledge of a music stand adjusted to exactly the right level. It counteracts the drooping position, and allows them to devote all their attention to the movements of the right hand and arm for the time being.

There is one thing to be said against this mechanical aid to position—that is, that children are apt to take to it too kindly, and continue it too long unless watched.

A good many small people have a rooted objection to pressing their fingers sufficiently hard upon the strings. If they are really musical, one can usually convince them that a hoarse and hazy tone is the inevitable result of such half-heartedness; but the lazy ones take a good deal of convincing upon the subject.

There are children, also, who do possess an averagely keen musical ear—proved by their singing or whistling in tune—who, yet, will not take the trouble to stop correctly or to alter a false note unless made to do so. With this goes a laxness in the matter of semitones.

If such carelessness is persisted in for an undue time, and in the face of constant reproof, the teacher is recommended to wash his hands of a thoroughly unsatisfactory pupil. He or she will never do anyone credit, and a player of that calibre, having possibly arrived at a meretricious semblance of proficiency after years of enforced grind, becomes a public nuisance and a private torture.

ON MUSICAL IDEALS.

I WONDER if we thoroughly realise the value of ideals—how they lighten many sombre lives and spur us on to achieve the seemingly impossible? If they are so mighty with us, men and women who have drunk deep of disillusion and disappointment, what magic may they not wield with little children, to whom is given such beautiful confidence in the untried future. But out of this very confidence arises the possibility of worshipping false gods, serving unworthy ideals, and it is our privilege, out of our more mature knowledge and experience, to help them to choose aright.

Much might be said concerning the deplorably materialistic atmosphere which pervades many homes, in which the only incentive to the acquirement of know-ledge, expressed or implied, lies in the prospect of ultimately "besting" your neighbour in place or prosperity. Needless to say, that is not the atmosphere which engenders ideals—though those who habitually breathe it point to apparently successful practical results. It produces smart, up-to-date workmen—but neither philosophers nor artists.

At present, however, we are only dealing with the question of musical ideals; how they may be suggested to the childish mind, and how the beautiful may be brought directly under his observation.

Some children are so naturally prone to idealise, that they will inwardly exalt the performance of the butcher's boy upon a comb, or a jew's harp, into some-

thing little less than divine. A poor sort of ideal, doubtless, but the interesting part is, they almost always
endeavour to imitate if not to excel the original performer—excellent proof of the stimulative power of
any ideal upon mind and capacity.

If teachers of the violin would only talk less and play
more to their little pupils, the process of instruction
might be made vastly more agreeable to both parties.
How is a child, who cannot yet experiment for himself,
to discover any virtue in perplexing bowings and tire-
some finger exercises if the pleasure resulting from
ultimate combination of these things is not early impressed upon his senses? And it is just as easy to play
something for him from time to time; something short
and tuneful, but truly artistic. Play it in your best
manner, too, if you wish him, consciously or unconsciously, to appreciate the niceties of phrasing. Put it to
him that the magic of the music lies in the mastery
of the bowing; that the pleasing emotions he ex-
periences whilst listening are conveyed to him by subtle
gradations and delicate qualities of tone colour. And all
this with as few words as possible ;—only being careful
not to play to him over long.

Some of you may say that the child is incapable of
appreciating this perfection of detail ; that he will be just
as pleased with a banal polka, if you rasp it out to him
with resinous cheerfulness. Well, so he will. And he
will go on preferring the polka all his days if he hears
nothing but that class of music, badly written and badly
played, for the greater part of his youth. Moreover,
when he grows up, he will be a frequenter of music halls
and smoking concerts, and will dote upon the refrains
of popular songs and the wit of halfpenny "comics,"
and become a nuisance to all reasonable society.

Children must be guided in their aspirations. For
one that has an innate sense of perfection, you will meet
ten that are crude, curious, ill-balanced little mortals ;
nevertheless, with plenty of latent possibilities if only
they be directed into desirable channels. It is this

matter of direction that lies largely in the teacher's hands. He cannot increase the receptive capacity of the pupil's mind, nor hasten the often tardy processes of mental digestion, but it is his clear duty to provide proper intellectual food.

Any music intrinsically poor and worthless of its class is unfit for intellectual nourishment; and in this category I would include those compositions which aspire to classical form, and fail of arriving at anything but mere laboured vagaries of notation. Such compositions will surely prejudice the taste and destroy the critical faculty of a pupil who is obliged to study them, and will, just as surely, reflect discredit upon the teacher who, of free will, selects such undesirable material for study.

If we honestly give the children of our best, in the days of their pupilage, they, in turn, will give of their best to the world when they grow up. And to have added to the sum total of good in the world—even in remotest and humblest manner—is no small thing to our comfort when the years begin to close in.

ON CONSISTENCY.

IT is impossible for teachers of the violin to over-estimate the importance of consistency in dealing with their little pupils.

The violin is an instrument of suggestion rather than of realisation. In the hands of the inexperienced it produces no musical sound but an intolerable noise. This peculiarity is not shared with keyed or fretted instruments, which, by reason of a more mechanical construction, occasionally produce tolerably pleasing effects under the fingers of happy chance. But the whole art of playing the violin is the outcome of intellectual and emotional understanding. The one faculty will not produce a true artist without due proportion of the other. If the teacher has sufficiently realised this in the course of his or her own training, it should have very practical influence on the manner in which he or she, in turn, imparts instruction—practical influence, in the resolute enforcement of certain necessary details of technique, and in the patience and care with which the necessity for obedience is made clear along with the demand. As an instance—firm and decisive stopping is absolutely requisite to the production of true and resonant intonation. Explain this law in as few and simple words as possible—then insist upon the observance of it.

Some children are of a singularly apathetic intellect; others, again, are quick enough to grasp your meaning, but do not remember what you have told them, and in some cases, fail to transmit the idea into experience.

Having once expressed your will on any matter, and made sure that it is understood, draw, if necessary, upon your entire store of patient determination in bringing about the desired result. Don't let the child weary you out. Some children have amazing powers of passive resistance, and if they are permitted to get the upper hand, through weakness or laziness on your part, you may as well give up the idea of teaching them the violin. Remember also—for your comfort, if you are of a philosophical turn—that you are not only influencing your pupils on present and special occasions, but building up in them a standard of values as to reasonable and unreasonable exhibitions of determination; awakening them to the force of active consistency as opposed to passive and unjustifiable resistance. For you are not only teaching them the violin during the hour or half-hour that they are in your company; you are adding your mite to the great constructive and formative influences of their lives. This is a very necessary view to keep before one during the long day's work—which is often peculiarly discouraging, and fatiguing to mind and body.

Mere musical knowledge and ability cannot, of itself, generate that gift or combination of forces which gives to the world a great interpretative artist. Moral as well as intellectual qualities must combine to such an end.

Do you think that *your* work has no affinity with such great aims? Are you consciously limiting your efforts by poor and narrow ideals, contenting yourself with common and apparent standards of achievement?

Aim at a star, and you will attain to the house-top. Suggest, aid and direct with every faculty at your command, and you will have done better work than you may ever see the limit of.

There is nothing more subversive of discipline, more inconsistent with the true end of it, than a perpetual and inconsequent use of the word "don't." The air is thick with "don'ts" in some houses and in some class-rooms; yet, those parents and teachers who so

continually utter it, frequently neglect to ensure any
practical result. Then they wonder why their children
and pupils are more unruly and disobedient than those of
other people:—" It is not for want of *telling*," they say,
" that the child went wrong."

Just so. You reproved him so continually that the
words lost all value and influence. You prohibited many
things, but you enforced abstinence from none. Yet,
you wonder that the child is disobedient.

Reduce your "dont's " to as small a family as possible,
but, once uttered, secure compliance with your command. If you have been just and equable in your
dealings, there will be no difficulty about the compliance; it is, in reality, a truer test of you than of
the child.

ON "FIRST APPEARANCES."

THIS has nothing to do with prodigies, or, indeed, with trained adult performers either amateur or professional. It is concerned only with the "first appearances" of the average small pupil, and the scene is probably the platform of a school or studio concert.

I should like to say a few words in favour of these juvenile concerts. They are not, on the whole, as tedious as some more ambitious entertainments, and they offer an unequalled occasion to fathers, mothers, aunts and cousins, to compare the progress of their particular hopeful with that of his fellow students, and with the pupils of other teachers. Also, to note his development, if any, between early and subsequent performances.

It may be taken for granted that nobody goes to these affairs with the expectation of hearing finished artistic renderings. On the whole, these audiences are more likely to over-rate technical skill and miss the less obvious germs of insight and individuality. This over-sight has a chilling effect on the children whose intellectual grasp is ahead of their executive ability. Public opinion has usually a great influence on childish minds, particularly the opinion of their immediate circle. If they hear: "Why, little So-and-so has only been learning two years, and he can play ever so much better than you, who have been five!" they feel aggrieved, and it is beyond them to retort that little So-and-so has more flexible joints and possibly a nimbler order of brain. They only know that they have honestly striven to reproduce whatever has appeared to them of pleasant or beautiful effect, and, as far as they can see, it has been labour wasted, since the majority of the listeners did not appreciate their efforts. It would be well if the few who *did* see that the less brilliant performer had possibilities, made known their opinion to him afterwards, in private.

It does not follow that the child who is slow to execute, and infinitely more difficult to teach in the initial stages, may not ultimately develop into a more interesting musician than the one who learns with facility, and to whom the knowledge, easily acquired, means no more than an opportunity for showing off his digital dexterity.

And here I have stumbled upon a possible objection to some results of these small-fry concerts. They *do* foster an objectionable amount of conceit in children who are naturally forward, and who are continually belauded by an admiring home circle.

In these cases the teacher must act as a judiciously applied brake upon the buoyancy of their advance. Let them see that other children excel them in particular instances, if not all round : the slow child brings perhaps a more beautiful tone, the awkward child possesses a finer ear, the nervous child more insight and sympathy. Be scathing upon their defects, but let them feel, nevertheless, that you expect great things of them. If they are of true metal they will labour the more earnestly to excel, and will, in time, cast their conceit as a husk by the way.

Nervousness does not, as a rule, hamper the younger pupils as much as their elders. It comes with the dawn of self-consciousness, the beginning of that state of "finding one's level" which persists for a longer or shorter period with all of us. The limit and extent of our powers once determined, we can proceed with modest assurance, but while we are still uncertain, and depend for our estimate on the report of other people, nervousness is a factor which must be reckoned with and counteracted by every possible means.

Never set a highly nervous child to play in public a piece which he can barely master in the privacy of his home. If he breaks down in a difficult passage (which he is almost certain to do) it will increase his nervousness tenfold, and the strain will probably have a bad effect upon his physical health.

The public performance of a highly strung artist is usually either a little below, or considerably above his average standard. The same holds good of a nervous child ; therefore it is better to choose something which, though he may not render it in his best style, he will, at least, play creditably. If he happens to play it above his usual average it is a charming surprise, but an incalculable quantity.

ON KEEPING UP THE INTEREST.

YES, that is where the difficulty comes in ; that is the test of your mettle. To keep up the interest, whilst you are superintending the exercising of unaccustomed muscles and bending obstinate little wrists into flexible curves. It is so monotonous, and tiring, and disenchanting, and seems to have so remote a connection with music, as they understand it, that it is no wonder if the little thoughts often wander and the little ears are closed to instruction.

And it is not only with the wee ones, but to a considerable extent with older pupils that this apathetic condition arises to thwart our efforts. So few of them are capable of realizing that the way of infinite pains is the best way, indeed, the only way, to the desired end ; that it is impossible to hasten these preliminary stages of bowing and fingering without jeopardising the entire framework of violin technique. They come to the lesson with laggard footsteps ; keep one eye on the clock and the other, warily, on your forbearance ; and when they shut your door at the close, they shut their minds on the subject—till the recurrence of the purgatory.

With the tiny ones this stage usually passes with the first weeks or months of training. We are taking for granted that the specimen under consideration is the average small child who forms the staple working-material of the provincial teacher, and whose parents have decreed that, willy-nilly, it shall learn the violin. (Pupils of more than average talent are a rare find, particularly with junior teachers.) Once, however, that the former has learnt to produce fairly agreeable sounds with tolerable ease, he is wont to improve steadily, sometimes even rapidly, and repay one for the anxieties of probation.

It is otherwise with the elder pupils. They, also, are subject to periods of inattention and retrogression, sometimes obviously accountable, sometimes not.

Among the accountable periods may be reckoned the close of the summer term, when atmospheric conditions incline us all to take things easy. The counter attractions of society, or of some special hobby, are also hostile forces in the field. But apart from these recognised causes, there are seasons when both pupil and teacher are conscious of a depressing and inexplicable lack of enthusiasm and spontaneity, when the violin lesson is merely a thing to be gone through with, and the interim practising is scant and perfunctory.

If you feel the remotest fear that you are drifting into the grey limbo of ineffectual things, pull up, and pull up sharply. Break new ground at once, if you value your ultimate peace of mind. Do not stop to think how it may look in the eyes of too conservative papas and mammas. Their uneasiness will dwindle according as their offspring's interest revives and his playing improves. Alter the order of your lesson, and the order of his study. Open to him new portals in the palace of sound; either by eye, by ear, or by some analogous quality of interest. Give him a fresh nut to crack, and make sure that he has faith in the kernel.

That faith in the kernel is the main thing with all of us, the hope that keeps us gritting our teeth on many a hard nut of progress or politics. Translated into the sphere of the violin lesson, it means simply attracting the pupil's attention sharply to some particular branch of his art, hitherto untouched, and proving to him, by conclusive personal demonstration, that the exercise of it is really a pleasant occupation; but one, nevertheless, which can only be enjoyed through intelligent effort and determination.

You cannot do this merely by sitting easily in your chair and talking about it.   You have got to influence that pupil by your whole personality; to lift him out of his apathy by sheer force of will.   It takes an effort to do this, often a very great effort, according to tempera-ment; but it leaves you with your own mind cleared, your own muscles braced for the battle.   Resolve on success.   Do not make a spurt and fail to sustain it. He who half tries and half succeeds, will fail altogether in the long run.

A teacher needs staying power just as a racer, or a political leader.   Thought produces effect by *impact*. Will produces thought by *impact* upon the grey matter of the brain.   Your mind will generate thought in another mind by *impact* of a direct and forceful stream of ideas. There is literal truth in the saying, "hammer it in." Drive not only your ideas, but the vital force behind your ideas into the mind that you are quickening to action.   There is no formula that will help you to attain this mastery, and no reflected light will direct your feet into the straight path; but guidance will come with the occasion, if only you have courage to seize it.

G

THE DULL PUPIL.

WHAT is to be done with the dull or unmusical pupil? It is a question which has many aspects, and which all of us, who are engaged in teaching the violin or kindred instruments, are constantly compelled to answer in some practical manner.

One solution of the difficulty—if you are convinced that his dullness is impenetrable—is, of course, to refuse to teach him; to declare that he has absolutely no receptive capacity; that you cannot waste your time pouring water into a sieve; and so forth. This is, probably, the first way of escape that suggests itself to the worried junior teacher, who has enthusiasm for his instrument and all his professional experience to get. But it is open to many objections. Firstly, it is an unqualified confession of failure; secondly, it is throwing away an excellent opportunity for testing various methods; and thirdly, it entails a loss of income.

Now, as to this last objection, there is no necessity to enter into too many particulars. All teachers may be presumed to require an income; and the too hasty rejection of pupils, on the score of stupidity, is almost certain to give offence to parents, who may have it in their power to injure you professionally in ways and places that you had not suspected. Even quite unintentionally and in good faith they may spread a report that you prefer to take "picked" or advanced pupils, and so prevent others applying for lessons for fear of a similar fate.

Concerning the first indictment:—that it is an un-qualified confession of failure:—you probably imagine that the failure is all on the other side. But are you quite certain? Have you really put forth all your energy; tried every *variety* of educational method known to you; endeavoured to grasp the child's mental attitude as well as to inculcate your own? Or have you clung too much to a hard and fast rule?

A child's obstinacy is long, but it is not everlasting; and once it goes, it goes completely. It is for you to assist the dispersion, to coax, cajole and wheedle the little sinner into a better frame of mind. Don't be afraid of losing your dignity; you can never do that if you are sincere and simple. There is much more likelihood of your keeping too much aloof; giving him dry-as-dust precept instead of pleasanter example. " Helping the lazy ones on wid a stick" *may* have effected redoubtable things in the time and the hands of Father O'Flynn, but it has gone out of vogue as an educational method, and is, decidedly, a forbidden " help" to the junior teacher. His or her only weapon is tact.

Learn the nature, the powers and weaknesses of every pupil before you say that you cannot teach him. Talk to him out of lesson time. Find out what he thinks about; what are his likes and dislikes. It may be that he is being " spoon-fed" in some other department of learning:—that is, that the exercise of his individual intelligence is not insisted on. This is an obstacle with which I frequently have had to contend. Neither parents nor teachers should put words into a child's mouth unless they are sure that the equivalent for them is in his understanding. This mere memorising—as a system of teaching—is, happily, obsolete; but one still meets some sad survivals, some dull and uninterested little specimens of its unfortunate results. They have got to be awakened; and it is a difficult process.

No one, however, can really play the violin without having all his faculties well on the alert. No other musical instruments are so absolutely dependent on individual effort as those of the fiddle family. Nothing about them is ready-made, mechanical. One comes, after long familiarity, to associate with them something almost of human sensibility, so sensitive and responsive are they, not only to physical, but to psychical atmosphere. It stands to reason, then, that they will yield no music to unsympathetic hands, no sweetness to flaccid minds and muscles. If, therefore, when you have honestly tried every means in your power, and have not been too readily discouraged, you perceive that the child has not made any real progress, any real start, perhaps, it is time to say, with sober conviction, "This child will never become a violinist." But do not say baldly and hastily that he is "dull" or "stupid." Give a definite reason, such as :—He cannot play because he has no sense of pitch ; or, because of some unusual conformation of the hands ; or, because he is lacking in certain qualities essential to a musician. Be the reasons what they may, clothe the objection—for your own sake as well as for his—in the terms that are least likely to rankle in the minds of either parents or pupil.

ON FINGERING.

I WONDER how many average amateur violinists, who have ceased taking lessons, take the trouble to finger their new music before actually beginning to practise it ? Not the majority, I fear—particularly if the piece is something that they have recently heard and are anxious to reproduce quickly, and with as little trouble as possible. A great many of the dainty and delightful little "encore" pieces played by our modern concert artists are victimized in this way by the unskilful imitator. All goes well enough, perhaps, except for "just one" passage; "just one" little bit that evades the player's grasp and worries him or her every time the piece is brought out. Yet, very often this worry and uncertainty is caused by having no fixed scheme of fingering. The performer attempts it in several different ways and sticks to none in particular. Now, it is quite right to finger it *at first* in various ways, but, after due consideration of the effects, a choice must be made and rigidly adhered to; otherwise there will be lasting confusion in the violinist's mind concerning that precise passage, and it will remain a permanent defect in what might otherwise be a meritorious rendering.

The safest plan is to mark every change of position in good, clear pencilling as soon as a definite choice has been made. It can be rubbed out later if desirable, but it should be left as long as there is the slightest hesitation in the stopping.

There are several considerations which must influence us in our choice of fingering. Roughly speaking, they may be classed under three heads: viz., Facility, Phrasing, and Tone-colour.

The term "Facility" is not altogether easy of definition without special illustration, because it so often happens that " one man's meat is another man's poison " in matters technical. Indeed, as regards fingering, the shape and size of the hands must often be taken into account as well as the speed and style of the music. Consequently we can only throw out a few general suggestions that may prove useful.

In lengthy ascending passages begin to shift early, and do not keep all the work for the E string.

In repetition of broken chord passages it is better to divide the notes between two strings, or more, and remain in one position, than to keep perpetually shifting.

In chromatic passages, choose one out of the accepted fingerings and stick to it. Variations of fingering in this scale are more likely to result in faulty intonation than even in the diatonic modes.

The understanding and practice of correct "Phrasing " is of the greatest importance to all true lovers of music. Without it, melody is pointless and tasteless, and harmony degenerates into mere tolerable noise. The violinist phrases with his bow as the singer with controlled breathing, and any manner of fingering which interferes with, or renders ineffectual, this special function of bowing must be unhesitatingly condemned. It may be conspicuously easier for the left hand to play certain notes in a different manner from that indicated or implied by the composer, but if the alteration seriously interferes with the spirit of the phrasing, then the apparent convenience is too dearly bought. Indeed, it is surprising how many thoughtless players sacrifice the greater to the lesser in this matter; get the notes anyhow and anywhere, with the faintest conception of the inartistic effect, and thus inflict indescribable suffering upon more sensitive musicians.

Very much the same reasoning applies in the consideration of "Tone-colour." Each string has its characteristic quality of tone; and in no case will notes produced upon the upper portion of one string sound exactly

similar if played upon the lower part of the next.
To take an instance with which, no doubt, you are
all familiar: how much finer and more sonorous the
opening melody of Raff's "Cavatina" sounds when
played altogether on the fourth string than when the
third and even second strings are utilised for the higher
notes! Again; the middle third of the D string is used
with excellent effect in parts of Wieniawski's "Legende,"
when the impression to be conveyed is that of a veiled
and mysterious melancholy. This peculiar quality of
tone could not have been obtained in any other register,
but it is not by any means the easiest way of playing
the notes. Once more, facility must be sacrificed to
phrasing; or in this instance, more particularly, to tone.

Of specific faults, that of using the open string where
a stopped note would be preferable is extremely
prevalent with children. It is commonly caused by
laziness—the dislike to exerting a weak fourth finger
when anything else can be substituted. Akin to this
is the habit of not stopping *any* finger sufficient firmly,
thereby producing a hoarse and hazy instead of a clear
note; also that of letting the thumb slip upwards with
a convulsive wriggle, when a note such as F natural on
the first string is required.

Harmonics, even the natural series, should, like the
open strings, be rather sparingly used. There are two
reasons for this; one—having chiefly reference to young
pupils—being that it is necessary to displace the lower
fingers in order to produce them; which displacement
should be avoided without good reason. The other
objection lies in the nature of their sound, which is
easily distinguishable from that of the surrounding
stopped notes, not having their fulness or intensity, but
being, by contrast, more clear and penetrating. Their
legitimate use depends entirely on the player's judgment,
but in a sustained scale passage they are usually undesirable. The treatment of artificial harmonics does not
come within the province of this paper.

ON MEMORISING STUDIES.

I WONDER how many students who try as a matter of course to memorise their pieces ever think of memorising their studies also, or whether they realise to what extent this exercise would benefit them in cases of obstinate technical difficulty?

There is so much time wasted in front of a violin-stand by students who have, so to speak, only a formal acquaintance with the second, fourth, and fifth positions, and who will never get any closer because, though they repeat the passages, or even the whole study many times over, there is all the while a sort of intangible veil between their minds and the eyes which follow the notes, and they are as uncertain at the end as at the beginning what exactly constitutes the difficulty which they cannot overcome.

Now, there are two principal sorts of difficulty to be met with in the left hand work of the general run of violin studies. First, the sort which only requires to be met by a measure of physical adaptability strengthened by habit, such as an extension or a rapid shake; and secondly, the sort which implies knowledge of the rules and combinations of fingering, and taxes the student's mind rather than his fingers. For instance, a study played throughout in a single position seldom contains anything very difficult for the fingers, unless it happens to be in one of the extreme positions; but, all the same, if it is written in the second, or fourth, it presents a mental obstacle which a lazy pupil instinctively shirks, and even the well-meaning finds inconvenient at first. But if the mental difficulty of considering the fingers in a new set of relationships is augmented by the addition of purely physical difficulties such as extensions,

sequential shifts, and skips, a much greater demand
will be made on the pupil's abilities, and it is in the hope
of rendering the mastery of such passages more feasible
and doing away with much vain repetition that I
suggest to the student the value of memorising certain
parts, or, better still, the whole study.

Perhaps an analysis of one or two of the best-known
studies with which the great majority of violinists must
almost inevitably be familiar, will prove useful in
illustrating exactly what I mean. Let us choose No. 13
out of Kreutzer's "Forty Studies" (Litolff). Except
in two instances it does not exceed the fifth position,
and at first sight the pupil who has just achieved No. 12,
or, at all events, essayed it, thinks he is in for an easy
time. But it does not always happen so, and with
the ninth bar his unexpected troubles begin. He is
never quite sure which finger is to fall on the first
note of the tenth or twelfth bars, and the fourteenth
is another stumbling-block. Bars 21-22, 27-28, 40, 41,
46 and 47, all contain elements of uncertainty for an
unsystematic practiser, and if he merely plays the notes
by sight, trusting to chance or a good ear to pull him
through, they are likely to remain in a parlous condition.

But if he turns his back to the stand and memorises
bars 9-10, and the rest in order, he will find that the
deliberate effort of recollection fixes notes and fingers
in their relative relationships in his mind and leaves him
no further difficulty to overcome except that of shifting
in tune. I purposely selected No. 13 as one containing
less obvious difficulties (as regards the left hand), than
some of the earlier studies, but No. 10, particularly in
the thirteenth and following bars, and the whole of
No. 12, can hardly be confidently played unless treated
in some such manner.

Needless to say, this applies also to more advanced
studies, and we will choose the next example from
among Rode's "24 Caprices." The fifth, sixth, seventh,
and eighth bars of the second Caprice consist of a
sequence of first inversions which are frequently played

out of tune, but which can easily be memorised if they are analysed thus;—Bars 5 and 6, first and second fingers close and semitone shift; bars 6 and 7, whole tone shift, second and third fingers close; bar 8, semitone shift, second and third fingers close. Bar 9 will require some repetition in order to give the *sforzando* B on the fourth string its due emphasis without coarseness. Bars 19-20, 25-27, 34-36, 42-46, all require to be analysed and then memorised in the same way as bars 5-6. This cannot be properly done without a knowledge of harmony, which is quite as essential to the violinist as to the pianist.

One of the benefits of this method is that the student can take his difficulties in small doses during spare moments, without having his music by him, and it is not so apt to dull the ear. He can also walk up and down the room, and so ease the strain of a fixed position; can even practise in the train if he happens to have a carriage to himself; can, in fact, make use of much valuable but disconnected time which would otherwise be wasted. This applies particularly to pupil-teachers or young professionals who are trying to combine performing with teaching.

Students differ very much with regard to their relative facility in memorising. To some it comes without effort, to others, only with difficulty, and to a few, it seems almost impossible to acquire. But none need despair. Determination and a definite system achieve wonders, and it is not outside the power of one of the latter class of students to perform an entire recital programme, containing sonatas as well as more melodic solos, without notes and with no more mental strain than is usually associated with affairs of the kind.

But this cannot be done in a hurry. The essential thing in the beginning is to take only a few bars at a time and to be sure that you are note- and finger-perfect in these before you go on.

Let us return once more to the Kreutzer Studies and experiment with the second. To the casual glance it

appears peculiarly difficult to memorise because it contains much repetition and apparently few or no salient
points. But instead of beginning at the beginning,
suppose we start at the latter half of the ninth bar.
We have here a succession of passages within an octave
which, if played in the first position, contain the first hint
of difficulty, *i.e.*, that of crossing strings without uneven-
ness. This is sufficient to fix the attention and provide
a motive for special study. We will therefore assume
that the pupil has mastered this passage up to the
latter half of the twelfth bar before going to those
following, in which the noticeable point is the regular
skip of a third in each ascending scale. This figure
continues up to the sixteenth bar, in which a fresh
one is introduced, lasting for two bars only. After this,
bar must be added to bar separately until the end is
reached, when it will be found comparatively easy to
memorise the beginning.

Treat your study like a landscape seen from a height :
take the notable features first—the hills, rivers, and
valleys,—then fill in surrounding details bit by bit.
Don't, as a rule, begin with the opening bars and
work straight through ; you don't get the same sense of
proportion in that way.

Two further hints may prove useful to the student :—
First take a precise mental photograph of the bar *as it
looks* in case your idea of the sound should not be trust-
worthy ; secondly, when you have considered each detail
of the passage, *trust your fingers.* Believe that they will
hit the bull's-eye at first shot, and in nine cases out of
ten you will be justified. Perhaps there is just one more
suggestion or recommendation which may profitably be
added, viz., when the student is about to perform in
public for the first time without notes, let him leave his
music in the dressing-room, because if it is anywhere
within reach of the platform he is liable to feel, suddenly,
that he cannot get on without it, while if it is practically
unattainable, he knows that he *must* get on, and
accordingly does.

THE STUDENT'S FIDDLE.

I SUPPOSE it is hardly necessary, in the present day, to remind the junior teacher to suit the size of the instrument to the stature of the pupil. In the dark ages of provincial violin playing—that is to say, twenty or more years ago—there was an idea prevalent that unless a child learnt from the start on a full-sized fiddle he would never acquire certainty of intonation; the alteration in length of stop being considered an almost insurmountable obstacle. This fallacy led to many a wearisome and unsatisfactory hour's practising, when childish body and mind alike rebelled against the unnatural strain. In addition it was responsible for numerous faults in position of the left hand and arm, as well as for much stiff and uneven bowing.

That day, however, has passed away; and we have cause to be thankful for it. The spread of local examinations—in touch with up-to-date central bodies—has brought a faint wind of progress into the dullest of country towns, and even villages " at the back of nowhere " can boast their contingent of little black cases, carried to and fro over many a long road to the nearest school or teacher.

That there *are* so many of these embryo fiddlers sometimes seems to be doubtful matter for congratulation—judging by the average quality of their performances. True violin playing comes only by intuition. There is a *something*, an indefinable quality in every innate violinist which lifts even faulty playing into a borderland of beauty : without that elusive something we may have tonality, rhythm, volume, irreproachable correctness, but

it is not violin-playing ; it is merely a performance on
the violin. Out of the many who stand forth to enter-
tain us, in public and in private, there are, alas, comparatively few who can at will lay cheek to fiddle
lovingly and draw forth that inner voice of delightful
melody, that song of the bygone forest and the winds
that hums at the heart of every fiddle thoughtfully
fashioned by the hand of man.

But we have wandered a long way from our little half
and three-quarter size instruments, waiting, in dusty
stacks, at the warehouse for the coming of the new pupil.

Now, from long and varied experience, I have dis-
covered that price is, in itself, no criterion of the musical
value of an instrument. The junior teacher will do well
to test this for himself, and I have no doubt that in time
he will discover that it is possible to get a good, an
indifferent, and a faulty instrument at exactly the same
price. There is an amazing individuality about even the
trade hacks, turned out wholesale by the hundred, and
apparently as alike as a regiment of tin soldiers. Try
nine or ten of them in succession : the sort marked
" Copy of Antonius Stradivarius," price 10s. You will
meet several that seem to be suffering from heavy colds;
others, with the voice of a fog-horn or a syren; one or
two with no voice to speak of ; and at the last, one with
quite an agreeable and fairly even tone. Buy it on the
spot.

Once upon a time a friend of mine bought just such a
fiddle to commence with. According as she improved
in her playing she wished to change it for a better-class
instrument, and, much to her surprise, was allowed 20s.
for it in the exchange. Later on, she met with it once
more, in the hands of a youth who was taking lessons
from the same master. And the youth's father had
given 25s. for it ! This, of course, is an exceptional
case, and the junior teacher is not recommended to
speculate in a stock of cheap fiddles on the strength of
it. It shows, nevertheless, the wisdom of careful selection in the matter of even a third-rate instrument.

The same diversity attends the choice of fiddles running from about £5 to £10. Matured instruments are always more desirable than new ones, but if the former are not immediately obtainable at the price, a violin which has been used for even two or three years is preferable to an absolutely untried one. A raw fiddle, like a raw horse, sometimes discovers unsuspected vices in course of training. These may be looked for more especially on the third and fourth strings, but the upper portions of the first and second should also be carefully tested for shrill or thick notes. Then, it is possible that the strings may be set too far apart for small fingers, consequently their position on the bridge will require alteration; or the height of the nut is not quite accurately gauged, and the fourth string jars against the finger-board. All these little matters should be rectified before putting the instrument into the pupil's hands, as he has sufficient difficulties to overcome in the natural course of study without being thereby set at a disadvantage.

Those fiddles of ancient fame, which are deeply coveted by all enthusiastic amateurs, are often priced out of all proportion to their musical value. Pedigree is a fine thing, no doubt; but condition and tone are of more practical importance to the player. There are many fiddles of uncertain ancestry which are to be had at less than half the price of their aristocratic cousins, and which will give quite as much satisfaction from the musical point of view. Unfortunately, if they bear sufficient resemblance to the work of any well-known maker they are frequently sold as authenticated specimens of the same by unscrupulous dealers. Hence we counsel the junior teacher never to buy a high-priced instrument, claiming to belong to a famous maker, without also receiving a written guarantee, signed by a reputable firm.

ON TEACHERS—SOME PORTRAITS.

HAVING dealt with all varieties of pupils at some length, it was suggested to me, by a youthful reader, that it was now time to turn to the teachers of the violin.

The suggestion commended itself upon reflection. If I had, to the best of my ability, indicated to the instructor how to influence and make the most of his material, it was only fair to the material to give it, individually, some hints towards making the most of its instruction. But the longer I considered the matter the more difficult the treatment of it began to appear, seeing that the pupil is, relatively, so very dependent on the teacher. A hunger for knowledge and a habit of obedience are, no doubt, the best aids to progress, but the minor virtues of punctuality and courtesy do wonders towards making the wheels run smoothly and accelerating the general advance. The pupil who wants to get on must, to some extent, study the teacher as well as the fiddle. Many men, many moods; and not all of them are propitious. Some students have intuition; others, none; needless to say, the former escape many awkward corners. But as no amount of co-operation on the student's part can make bad teaching good, I shall endeavour to point out some of the defects and weaknesses most likely to be met with on the lower rungs of the professorial ladder.

As I take up the pen, there passes before my mind's eye a long procession of familiar faces, some old, some young; some confident, others weary; but all, alike, associated with those suggestive little cases that may enshrine anything from a Strad to the veriest ear-

torturer. How, out of so many, to choose the typical
few for my gallery was the question. But when I
remembered that these papers were chiefly concerned
with the junior teacher, his difficulties, hopes and
aspirations; and that when he comes to be a senior
teacher he will have learnt in the school of life many
more things than I can tell him, and will have his own
gallery of remembrance to meditate in at the cool of the
day, I determined to pick my portraits from the full
ranks of the juniors, in the hope that he may meet
acquaintances and ponder profitably thereon.

And now, though I have for convenience sake used the
masculine pronoun, the junior teacher is, as a matter of
fact, usually feminine ; and our first portrait is that of a
girl.

She is very young, hard-working, and enthusiastic.
Her family being in straightened circumstances, she
cannot afford to finish her musical course without
beginning prematurely to teach. Studying towards her
diploma, the violin is in her hand at every available
moment, and her thoughts run unvaryingly in a groove.
She hopes to be a performer, and the teaching is a mere
interlude—a disagreeable interlude, except for the pay ;
and her method is dry and perfunctory.

Sometimes it happens that she fails in her examination.
That is a turning-point. Either she takes stock of her
powers and intentions and makes a fresh start on wiser
lines, or gets disheartened and gives up striving ; in
which case the teaching becomes even more unsatisfactory than before.

Be warned in time, poor little toiler! shake your
thoughts out of the rut and try to find some interest in
the outside world, especially in your pupils. Comparatively few—indeed, very few—attain to any eminence
as concert violinists, while many make a reasonable
income out of teaching. Pass on into the shadows,
No. 1, and let us make acquaintance with No. 2.

This young lady is of a more equable disposition. She
has passed all her examinations and her brain is

crammed full of maxims and definitions. She yearns for pupils, to teach exactly as she has been taught, not a pin's point of difference in the breadth of a crescendo or the fraction of a rallentando. She is conscientious and kind, and some of her pupils do excellently, up to a certain point; but with those of another temperament she can make no progress whatever. Pass on, No. 2: we have met you pretty frequently, and while we admire your good qualities we deplore their inelasticity.

No. 3 is a man; nor has he really any right to pose as a junior teacher, for he is of full age to have reached his artistic and intellectual level. But he " took up music," professionally, after he had tried his hand at a good many other things and failed. He has had no specialised training; probably has a little money, not sufficient to live on:—and he fiddles with a stiff wrist and an execrable tremolo. He takes pupils, too; not only for the violin but for several other instruments; and he has gained a reputation for getting them on rapidly. One finds them, indeed, playing sentimental melodies and scraps of Italian opera before they have mastered the scale of C, or learned to draw an even bow from nut to point. They are quite often budding geniuses; such prodigies, in fact, that the master early tells the delighted parent that he can teach them nothing more. It is probably true.

Our last portrait, like the first, is of an enthusiast. He, too, desired to be an executive artist, but the stuff was not in him; and when he was convinced of it, he wasted little time in vain regrets but set to work to find out what he *could* do. And he found that he could teach. Therefore he taught with heart and brain; felt his way, and tested many methods and systems; made mistakes and gained experience from them; felt tired and discouraged sometimes, but plucked up heart and fought on again. And to-day his pupils—to be found in many posts of honour and responsibility—look back and bless the name of the little master who helped them so devotedly along the uphill road.

H

ON HOLIDAYS.

"DEAR ME!" says the conscientious student, "what can this, possibly, have to say to the violin?"

Well, my friend, it has considerably more to say to it than you imagine. Indeed, sitting as I am this moment in the heart of a clover field, listening to the bees humming happily at the honey bags and the larks weaving spirals of song between heaven and earth, I know that I should be doing a great deal more good than preaching if I could only load a few hundred industrious students on a magic carpet and transport them into the midst of it; or scatter them, let us say, a few fields off; for it is the solitude and the murmurous stillness that is so healing and so wholesome.

But they must dust their minds clear of musical cobwebs, and let the sweet wind have free play in the musty corners, for it is little or no good to give the fingers rest unless the brain has rest also. Besides, knowledge ripens in silence. You may practise a study or a solo daily, hourly, a thousand times, with no result save infinite weariness and discouragement; but put it by for a while, and the understanding of it will grow slowly, imperceptibly, within you, until, on returning to the struggle, the fingers do, of themselves, what you strove in vain to effect in time past.

Some intelligences move more slowly than others, and it is useless to hurry them beyond their capacity. Nature will not haste for all your hectoring. But come to her humbly and trustingly, and she has ways of teaching that are infinitely more sure and satisfying than are the elaborated systems of men. Nature seldom or never specialises. All her arts, crafts, and sciences are allied, interpenetrable. She plucks you blossoms of joy from off the tree of pain, and teaches you by means of sternest life to play more whole-heartedly. And as the fields will not bear good yield of the same crop in successive years, so the human brain will yield sparse fruit and poor if it is sown too often with the same thoughts and ploughed in the same furrow. Change, freshness, wide culture—all these are necessary to the violinist who would be more than a mere drudge.

For music is not a branch of manual labour ; it is the rhythmical language of the universe ; the voice of things dumb ; the soul of things unseen. He who trudges in a perpetual round of scales, studies and prescribed solos, how can he put any fresh life into his music ? He has no influx of outward and varied experience. His road is narrow and straight, and runs between high walls. But let him only open a door and go out upon the hillside. Let him forget for a space that he is he ;—that Rode ever wrote caprices or Wessely compiled scales ;—let him stand, agaze and glad, as a little child in a field of flowers. And when he turns again to the narrow road there will be a new clearness in the old notes, a sweeter lilt in the well-worn phrases.

In cases where direct recourse to nature for rest and inspiration is difficult of attainment, an alternative study of different character, or even a purely recreative hobby, is of importance to the student, as affording the necessary mental variety. I cannot sufficiently impress upon enthusiastic students that the study of music, alone, will never make them *great* musicians. (I purposely reject the word *artist*, as it has frequently of late been asso-ciated with performances of solely technical interest).

It is the keenness of competition, not for a com-petency, but for affluence, which gives rise to so much over-practising, wrecked health, and stunted individuality. What is the value of ephemeral wealth and popularity if

H 2

the possessor is, humanly speaking, a loser thereby?
Undoubtedly, the gilded laurels are very tempting to the
majority of violinists ; but high tides ebb swiftly, and the
performer who depends upon *tours de force* for his success
is liable at any moment to be passed in the race. To
"hasten slowly," as the wise Latin proverb has it, is
indisputably the better course, and the bringing of all the
gifts and capacities to natural maturity is eventually
productive of a much finer creature than the forcing of a
particular talent to abnormal luxuriance. Unfortunately,
the tendency of the age, and of its economic conditions is
to grudge the time necessary for all-round development ;
but somewhat in the right direction may be done by
students for themselves, if they only grasp the central
idea ;—that a minimum of rest and variety is absolutely
essential to growth.

There are some violin students who, on reading this
apotheosis of rest and variety, will feel it in instinctive
harmony with their private desires and sentiments.
They will receive it as a heaven-sent message, and put it
into immediate practice. But it is not meant for them.
No, it is sent to the student who does not desire it ; who,
indeed, repudiates it angrily; wishing, only, to go on
practising as long as those poor slaves, his fingers, can be
spurred into action by a masterful will. And when his
body is tired out, and he must, perforce, cease playing,
his mind has not the vitality to project itself into a fresh
atmosphere, but jogs along, by tones and semitones, even
in his sleep.

Yet, in the busiest cities there are green and quiet
corners for those who would sit awhile apart; there is
the refuge of books, written in many tongues and reflect-
ing many personalities ; there are worlds of colour, of
human intercourse, of philosophy and speculation; all
these await only the opening of the door in the narrow
way, that way that grows even more narrow, more dusty,
as the days pass by.

ON ACCOMPANISTS.

A MID a plethora of pianists, a really good accompanist is sufficiently rare as to occasion profound thankfulness when one does light upon a genuine specimen.   Violinists have suffered even more than singers at the hands of unintelligent performers, as in the case of songs the words afford a simple key to the spirit of the composition.

The music of a violin is something like the foliage of a creeper—it needs a prop, a foundation to spread upon ; its tendrils are too slight and fine to brave the buffeting winds alone.   But unlike the creeper, which flourishes equally upon shapeless pile or Gothic arch, the music thrives only upon that structure which is adapted to its peculiar needs; and in this case the accompanist is the builder.

But they *will* build in their own way, these accompanists.   Their houses are not erected " to suit the taste of purchaser," as the ingratiating notice-board has it, but are unaccommodating mansions of a severe uniformity— that is, the majority of them are.   Let us be thankful for the exceptions !

The primary virtue in an accompanist is one of the rarest in society : it is the quality of unselfishness.   Perhaps " selflessness " would be the truer word, if it did not almost suggest colourlessness ; but the actual accompaniment must never be limp or ineffectual.   It should be comrade to the solo—more than that, true mate to it ; supplementing its weaknesses, covering its deficiencies, and heightening its excellencies.   And as it happens, the

piano is by no means the most sympathetic medium for
the display of these gifts.   It is not of the same family
as the violin, nor so sensitive in temperament, and it
lends itself much more readily to banal treatment.

Now, violin playing is rarely mediocre; it is either
positively disagreeable or decidedly pleasing.   It possesses to the full the quality of unexpectedness—and it
is this very point which the rank and file of accompanists overlook.

They think that when they play the notes correctly,
and pay reasonable attention to the explanatory words
and signs on the printed page, they are fulfilling the
whole duty of accompanists.   But it is not so.   That is
the merest letter of the law.   If one put no more into
the music than the page offers to the eye, then, indeed,
the kingdom of sound would be the poorest royalty upon
earth.   It is precisely the understanding and interpreting
of the *unwritten*, of that subtle spirit which can be no
more than hinted at with the indifferent aid of ink and
paper, that marks out the instinctive musician from his
fellows, and is, above all, the characteristic of the ideal
accompanist.

It is not obligatory to possess a very large amount of
technical ability, but on the other hand, a knowledge of
fingering is indispensable, as is also some acquaintance
with the earlier rules of harmony.   In fact, practical
harmony—not a mere affair of book and pencil—is an
invaluable aid to anyone who practises reading at sight.
By means of it the content of a bar is seized *en bloc*
instead of separately and disconnectedly, and difficult
passages can be temporarily condensed.   To violin
students, also, who are studying arpeggios of dominant
and diminished sevenths, it is of the utmost importance
to have a clear understanding of chord construction and
of key relationship.   Unfortunately, in many general
schools, and in some smaller music schools, harmony is
considered and taught as such a remote and dry-as-dust
subject that students naturally shirk it at the earliest
opportunity.

To return to the violin:—It is in the matter of *mezzo-piano* playing that the latent incompatibility between it and the piano is most apparent. Sonatas, ancient and modern, are full of such passages, in florid counterpart, in which the two are as it were engaged in confidential conversation, each in turn taking up the parable. At such times, inexperienced pianists almost invariably overpower the slighter instrument, and the composition sounds proportionately ill-balanced and weak. Delicacy of touch is especially desirable, and the acquirement of a really good style of phrasing; but alas! no amount of advice or instruction will impart the necessary understanding unless the player is inherently sympathetic.

It is an error to think that small children or backward pupils do not require an accompanist as much as elder or more advanced ones. They need, on the contrary, to be familiarised from the start with their pieces as a whole; otherwise, they are sure to make many mistakes when they do come together with the second instrument. Then again, the harmonic basis is a great help to those students who are not perfectly safe on the score of tune. Modulating passages which, when practised alone, often sound strange and even unmeaning to the untrained ear, become quite intelligible when taken over their proper bass, or the full modulating chord.

Now and again it happens that even violinists of considerable training, who have been studying by themselves some piece of unusual tonality, rhythm, or phrasing, find, on coming to try it with the piano, that they have totally misinterpreted it in general or particular aspects. The discovery is discouraging, but it should awaken them to the prompt necessity of seeking an accessible and reliable accompanist. Music composed for more than one instrument cannot be artistically comprehended in isolation, and the study of the work as a whole should precede the practising in parts.

GOOD TASTE IN MUSIC.

A S a matter of fact, a genuine taste for anything cannot be imparted by extraneous methods, but if it is pre-existent it can often be modified, to a certain extent, by circumstances. A taste for music, for instance, must be born with the individual, but the quality of it is frequently dependent on surroundings, or in other words, on education. A taste for music, again, does not necessarily imply an aptitude for all branches of performance. An excellent pianist may be a very indifferent violinist, or vice versa, and it sometimes happens that a really gifted singer has but the slighest acquaintance with the characteristics and capabilities of any impersonal instrument.

Much of what passes as a love for music is, in reality, a very mixed sentiment.

A man hears a band playing a popular waltz, or a stirring march, or a selection from some well-known opera, and he is moved to tenderness, to martial ardour, or to scenic remembrance, not so much by the actual music as by the associations which it calls forth in his mind. He listens gladly, and because certain quite unrelated emotions are agreeably excited thereby he volubly proclaims himself a lover of music. But music has really played only a very subordinate part in the matter. It has simply been the medium by which several quite separate and distinct ideas were suggested to his consciousness, just as the passing breath of some rare perfume will poignantly recall the remote company and occasion on which we first enjoyed it. But we do not, for such reason, proclaim ourselves lovers of perfume, and he to whom some wandering melody has purveyed a passing joy has no more fundamental right to proclaim himself a lover of music.

The true lover is he for whom each phrase, each lingering chord exhales its own most intimate aroma; to whom it brings not the suggestion of outward images but an abstract and impersonal pleasure, an emotion in itself complete and satisfying. But this purity of taste is seldom recognisable in early childhood. Children imbibe knowledge more naturally by methods of association. Music descriptive of some concrete fact—of the rocking cradle, the whirring wheel, or that illustrating the general sentiment of some little verse appended—is of the sort best calculated to awaken feelings of interest in the childish mind.

There is, comparatively speaking, a dearth of such music for tiny violinists; the little pianists are catered for more abundantly; but, even when teaching by associative methods and appealing most frankly to the pupil's imagination, it is possible, for stimulative purposes, to isolate a phrase, or an unusual chord, and endeavour to awaken an appreciative perception of its peculiar qualities. You may, or may not, be successful in the attempt, but it is worth trying; and the presence or absence of the power implied will make all the difference to the pupil's future musical development.

The average run of violin students are just on the borderland with respect to this matter, and it is difficult with them to tell a mere conventional assent from a real conviction until time has proved its worth. But time does tell, and that by means of their growing preference for pieces either of greater artistic excellence or of a showy and commonplace kind. The tendency towards these last must if possible be checked; but as the children are largely influenced by what they hear in the home and among their intimate circle, it is next to impossible to implant a genuine love for the beautiful amongst those who are in daily contact with low standards of musical taste. If the father of the family prefers to listen to the latest ditty from the '*alls*, or a quavering Sankey hymn tune fished out by ear on his daughter's fiddle, it stands to reason that the danghter's ear, being accustomed to such worthless stuff, will rapidly become deadened to all finer possibilities. Or even if the standard is one degree above this, and the " Holy City " and the waltz from the " Merry Widow " are substituted for the earlier programme, there will still be a difficulty in awakening any understanding or appreciation of more intellectual music, —unless, perhaps, it be of such universal acceptance as Raff's immortal " Cavatina " or Thomé's " Andante Religioso."

Fortunately, as I have said elsewhere, the violin lends itself less readily than some other instruments to this species of debasement. It is an aristocrat, even under compromising circumstances. Compare the Irish Jig or Scotch Reel played by the blind fiddler at the curb with the performance of the piano-organ in the next street. Is there not a difference which goes deeper than mere quantity and degree; a hint, on the one side, of a soul struggling for recognition, of the personality of a *Paragôt* against that of a potman? Nay, I will go further— Have you never heard a poor, threadbare tune, redolent of tawdry sentiment, suddenly touched to a strange significance by the hand of some half-starved fiddler, dreaming for the moment of things beyond ken. . .?

But that is the rare moment, and we come back to the ordinary hours of life in which, if we would keep them up to a certain level, we must consciously surround ourselves with the best, musically and artistically, that it is in our power to acquire. Let us then make sanctuary in our hearts for the most inspiring thoughts, the noblest poems, and the fairest pictures that they may dwell beside the loveliest melodies and keep us apart from all putative art that is insincere, common or unclean.

Appreciation grows by being charily fed, and though we may find less to approve we shall have keener satisfaction in the little. Undiscriminating partiality has no zest and is no spur to achievement. Matthew Arnold, in

his " Essays on Criticism " says, relative to good taste in
poetry, that our touchstone should be the most beautiful
lines and expressions of the great masters, and that
all effort which falls short of that quality of excellence
should be put aside as unworthy.   May we not apply the
same test with as good result to our taste in music?
It has nothing in common with formalism or a manner of
slavish imitation, but requires only that the aim be
sincere and the expression adequate, choice of material
and treatment being absolutely at the will of the artist,
subject to these fundamental conditions.   It is certain
that if the value of such tests were more widely
recognised we should be saved from much of the
puerility and insignificance which, under the name of
music, at present finds its way into the shops, and into
the homes of an uncritical public.

THE IMPORTANCE OF BOWING.

THERE is nothing connected with violin playing of such paramount importance as the acquirement of a really good style of bowing. Left hand technique is all very well, but it loses much of its artistic value when not joined to efficient right hand work. Bowing is responsible for the voice of the violin—apart from structural capacity—and a performance of the most brilliant cadenza, though it be phenomenal in speed and unerring in accuracy, lacks half of its possible effect if not enunciated with the proper phrasing and gradations of tone. The significance of correct bowing must be realised from the start by both teacher and pupil, and no pains should be spared in imparting, and making sure that the pupil understands, the fundamental principles of the art.

There are, of course, certain peculiarities in holding and manipulation associated with the different schools of playing at home and abroad. It is not my purpose, here, to advertise the excellence of any particular elevation or depression of elbow and forearm, or exact position of the right thumb;—equally good and useful work has been done by schools of very opposite doctrines in these matters;—but there are two essentials which professors of all schools are agreed upon, viz.: the necessity for cultivating a flexible wrist, and the power of drawing a straight and even stroke from end to end.

With regard to flexibility, young children are, as a rule, naturally adaptive from the physical point of view; to get them to understand and remember the exact

motions required is another affair, and one in which any
laxity or ambiguity on the teacher's side is attended with
disastrous consequences. One is only too apt to flag in
the persistent effort sometimes necessary to enforce the
proper application of rules on careless or obstinate little
children; to hope, unjustifiably, for the best instead of
making sure that one is actually on the road to it. But
trivial faults and irregularities, easily drifted into at this
stage, are extremely difficult to overcome later, and may
seriously interfere with the student's progress. It is
most disheartening to the adult, on going to a more conscientious teacher, to be put back to rudiments instead
of proceeding steadily up the hill of difficulty as he had
expected, and it has been responsible for total cessation
of the study on the part of more than one student who
might, under happier circumstances, have developed into
a promising player.

Every violinist finds the extremities of the bow the
most awkward to control, and for this reason the particular manner of changing the stroke at nut and point
should be practised separately, not too long at a time,
but very thoughtfully. Continuity of sound should be
aimed at, and approximated to as nearly as possible.
Harshness and weakness should alike be avoided.
Rigidity of the thumb and first finger joints will almost
invariably produce a most unpleasant roughness of tone
at the nut, the same defect being noticeable if too great
weight falls on the hair, either from a forearm active
when it should be quiescent, or from an unfortunate
arrangement of the fingers on the stick.

Change of stroke at the point is often very feeble and
ineffectual, the sound being not only reduced in volume
but sometimes quite changed in character. Here, again,
skilful manipulation of the first finger and thumb is of
the greatest importance in supplying the force necessary
to preserve a due balance of tone. The pupil has to
take into consideration not only that the point of contact is further from the controlling power (the right
hand) but that the stick itself tapers and becomes lighter

in this direction. It is one thing to perceive this with
the eye, but quite another to apply the knowledge of it
to the production of tone. I have met some fairly
advanced students who did not appear to have realised
it, and whose tone, in cantabile passages, very evidently
suffered thereby.

This leads us directly to the consideration of the
second essential—that of controlling the balance of tone
in drawing very slow strokes.

First of all, the stroke must be what is somewhat
misleadingly called straight—that is, the right arm, when
fully extended, should present no inward curve at the
elbow. (This, of course, does not apply to unusually
long arms, and must only be taken as a general direction).
Secondly, the pressure of the fingers must be minutely
graduated to correspond with the weight of the bow ;
and thirdly, the amount of stroke used should be carefully calculated with reference to the speed and proportionate volume of the notes required. This does not
pertain to the earlier stages of violin playing ; all that
can be done then is to prepare the way by insisting on
the daily practice of straight steady bowing, the note
being sustained to greater length according as the pupil
gains facility.

It is not a bad plan to set a metronome to, say, ♩. 50,
and to increase the duration of the note by degrees, a
couple of beats at a time, till the pupil arrives at a
considerable sustaining power. Failing a metronome,
the teacher probably counts ; but with the best of
intentions the oral beat is apt to vary day by day, and
does not, in consequence, furnish nearly so reliable an
estimate of progress as the mechanical one. The use of
a metronome also, as a test in certain stages of study
and sonata practice, is strongly recommended to both
elementary and advanced students—particularly to those
who have little or no chance of concerted playing—as
they are sometimes inclined, unconsciously, to adapt the
tempo to their immediate convenience in the more difficult
passages.

The bow, itself, requires to be selected, and not left altogether to the discretion of the vendor or the chance of a "complete student's outfit." Amongst these cheap articles one meets some with faulty screws, and more with warped sticks and sundry other defects of construction. Naturally, at the price, one cannot look for anything very fine in the way of balance, but it is well to avoid the worst specimens by testing them prior to purchase.

ON ORIGINALITY.

"People are always talking about originality; but what do they mean? As soon as we are born the world begins to work upon us, and this goes on to the end."—GOETHE.

"THE world begins to work upon us . . ."—aye, and according to the depth and distinctness of the impression are we of the true stamp or false coin. But this word "originality" is of most misleading utterance in the mouths of many. It is frequently cousin-german to "new," almost synonymous with "novelty," having grievously lost touch with "origin," its parent; which is no more, indeed, than "the world beginning to work upon us" or ever we are conscious of the world.

The violin, as an artistic product and so far as its structure is concerned, has steadfastly resisted innovation. From time to time various experiments have been made, either with the whole instrument or in part, and these having been tested, and even apparently approved by competent critics, have passed from brief notice to oblivion. Nor has the method of producing its music altered proportionately with the methods applied to other instruments of reed or percussion. It has acquired an extended scale, but the manner of tone production is substantially the same as in its infancy. Truly, it may be said that the violin is not only the aristocrat but the most conservative of all instruments, and constitutionally opposed to all cheap trickery and quack advertisement.

To be original, in the true sense, is to present the most faithful record of life's handiwork that we are capable of; *not* to paint the rose; to deck our thoughts, musical or otherwise, in startling phrases snatched by cunning hands from uncongenial quarters and grouped together, daringly, just as a smart milliner "creates" a hat. That implies dexterity, smartness; talent, if you will; but originality is at once a greater and a simpler thing.

Many times that our teachers of harmony and composition tell us to be, before all things, original, if they only told us to be sincere we should be nearer to a true conception of the matter. It is in the single-minded service of first perceiving and completing a beautiful and inspiring idea, and secondly, of presenting it vividly and consistently to the world, that originality, that genius itself, is conspicuously manifested.

The relation of our violin professors and pupils to the subject of discussion is somewhat different from that of the composition students. The attempts at individual expression of the former are, indeed, often in more danger of being overlaid than over-stimulated. And it is, to the majority of violin students, so much easier to imitate the teacher's manner—even unconsciously—than to devote personal criticism to the work of interpretation, that they acquiesce, as a class, in the more or less machine-made process of education.

The mischief begins with the abuse of a very excellent practice; that of teaching children rather by playing for them often and carefully than by overmuch theoretical instruction. There is no surer way of inspiring them with a real appreciation of what is fine or delicate, *but* beware of exacting an emotional duplicate of the performance. Are you so sure that you have no slight mannerisms or characteristics, not unpleasing or unfitting in *you*, because they are the natural exposition of your temperament, but which would prove unmeaning and awkward in one of different constitution? Don't think that because a child *is* a child he has no instinctive

I

artistic preferences, or that it is always obstinacy which prevents him from reproducing effectively on his violin the spirit of what you have played to him so earnestly and so often. Perhaps he is phlegmatic whilst you are vivacious; or gay and adventurous whilst you are contemplative; in either case, it is useless to expect him to enter easily into your frame of mind or to respond as readily as one of similar disposition. It is necessary to be content if he renders the general atmosphere of the study or piece without insisting on particular shades of expression, if you find that it does not come naturally to him to do so. This is not an admission of laxity. What the child *can* play and understand, let him feel that it is expected of him to do correctly and intelligently; but you cannot make a poet out of a grammarian, or a Sarasate out of an average stolid Briton.

On the other hand, a really gifted pupil may spontaneously improve on your reading, may even reach at an inspired leap the inner meaning of something of which you had unwittingly touched but the surface. That is the crucial moment for you both. If you have the insight and courage to recognise his superior gift and henceforth to support and supplement rather than to dogmatise, all will be well; but if you fail to perceive the relative values, and attempt to impose your triter reading on his finer intelligence, you will dull the keen edges of his sensibility and fill him with a torment of thwarted instincts; and when he leaves you—as he is sure to do in time—for a more catholic teacher, there will be a bitterness of misunderstanding on both sides that is not without effect on the whole character.

Those who are familiar with the story of Ole Bull (*Memoir* by Sara C. Bull), will remember the episode of the Swedish violin master in Ole's early days, and how, after the boy's amazing untaught performance of a Paganini Caprice, he said to him, complacently, "If you practice you may even come to play as well as I do."

Ole, even then, had his doubts!

It is a sort of thing which should not be unadvisedly

said to the most uninspired pupil. Children have often a juster estimate of character than their elders. They take your words *au pied de la lettre* and judge your actions accordingly ; and goodness help you if you promise more than you can decently perform ! Remember that the violin has moods as well as its master. There are days when, do what you will, it refuses to be coaxed into good humour ; and it is surely on those very days that certain small critics are most alert and attentive ! They may not speak, but every harsh or imperfect note is reflected in their disapproving small faces. . . But, have they not sufficient faith to understand if you say to them : "That was bad. You must do better"? The relations between you are not what they should be if it is impossible.

Moreover, it is the atmosphere of insincerity and the setting up of sham values when first "the world begins to work upon us" that blurs the stamp and leaves us ever shapeless and unfitted to high purposes. Expediency is no god for the children ; no god for us all ! His tools are soft and turn in the hand, and his image is mean and worthless. Better that pain and loss and labour should smite upon our hearts with ineffaceable strokes, than that we go down to the grave with a life half lived, a soul half starved, and eyes that have seen no harvest.

ON WASTE OF TIME.

I SUPPOSE many of you have learnt, in the course of your journey through life, that it is the busy man, the one who habitually puts in a vigorous and responsible day's work, who most often finds time for just that little extra which helps to ease the burden of a friend. The man who has what is known as a "soft job," or "something to keep him going," is very apt to spread it thin over a wide area; letting it, as it were, leak into his leisure, and thereby losing the true savour of either work or play. Moreover, he continually complains of lack of time when lack of method is really at the root of the matter.

To apply this to our music:—It is quite possible to keep one's fingers employed in practising for a period, two-thirds of which is absolutely valueless; it is equally possible to apply half one's mental energy to some study for half a day and be no wiser at the end of it, quality being relatively so much more important than quantity.

Practising the violin is fatiguing, mentally and physically, and the amount performed daily should be in proportion to the constitution, mental and physical, of the student. Too many teachers—and those by no means the least able—are apt to consider the pupil as a mere receptacle for their own knowledge, oblivious of his individual needs and capacity, and cram him with accomplishments beyond his powers of digestion. The result is unsatisfactory to both parties, and they do not always perceive the cause. But to continue practising when body and mind are overstrained is waste of time—worse than that, abuse of time. And it is the earnest and promising student who is most apt so to defeat his own ends; though none could feel more surprised or aggrieved on being told of it! The calisthenics of Sevcik, Wilhelmj, and other specialists of technique are excellent products of their kind, but they are only a few ingredients out of many that go to the making of a musician, let alone to the making of a man: yet how often violinists of delicate frame and temperament sacrifice themselves, with pathetic courage, in the attempt to compress into a strenuous week what nature had designed to be accomplished in three or four. And even supposing the goal to be attained, the objective speed, strength, or grasp to be really acquired, it has often been at the cost of undue physical expenditure, of all purely artistic refreshment, and of an increasingly false estimate of what genuinely constitutes a great artist.

A highly-strung sensitive student is not well advised to spend as many hours per day in technical practice as one of more placid temperament, for what he gains in dexterity he loses in intelligence and freshness. Even the phlegmatic student becomes heavier and more colourless for lack of variety, and it profits either of them little to become mere fiddlers—even virtuosi—if they are thereby isolated and out of touch with the manifold intellectual interests of the non-musical world.

The misapprehension of treating technical ability as an end rather than as a means lies at the root of much of this wasted time. That a measure of digital dexterity is necessary to a fitting exposition I grant you; but what avails it if there is nothing to express?—if the springs of interest and understanding are dried up for want of nourishment?

When we flock to listen to a great violinist we go with the hope of hearing something which will inspire us to better and more fruitful work in our several ways; something that, because of the world-wide spirit which is behind it, is common to us all, and is helpful and invigorating, alike, to those concerned in very different pursuits. But, alas! we often go away unsatisfied. We have listened to very perfect notes, very polished mechanism of music; but it has been music in its narrowest sense, highly interesting to the professional few, but cold and barren to the non-professional many. Music, as a profession, is studied too narrowly, too remotely. It is but one facet of a quintuple column, at the apex of which is Supreme Beauty. Well for the musician and well for the world if his strains are dyed with the painter's colours and rhymed with the poet's dreams. Well for him if we carry away with us a vision of mountain peaks lit with eternal sunrise, and abundently well with the world, since beauty is born of beauty. Alas, how rare are such blessed hours! We go hungry, for what?—perhaps we know not: but we know that we come away empty.

It is given to but one or two in a generation to be great artists, but the multitude is salted with those who can appreciate greatness, who have just so much of the gift of gifts as to depreciate bedizened littleness. To them we say:—Be jealous of your time, for it is irredeemable. When the brain flags give it rest; not necessarily in idleness, but with the ease of fresh diet. When the body flags give it rest; and turn the mind upon some new interest. If mind and body require rest together, it is because you have used them ill, and starved them of their natural nourishment.

It is in the student days—the growing time, which might be so happy and so beautiful—that one must begin to understand this. Once out in a hungry world, necessity too often lays a grasping hand upon the ordering of our hours, and if we have not learnt some of the secrets of freedom we are enslaved, before we know, to the god of the Highest Price.

The almost daily advent of startling innovations and inventions in matters of transit and of foreign communication has, no doubt, had its effect on the public appetite for things new and surprising in art (so-called) ; and in no department has this desire for mere novelty been pushed to greater length than in that of violin playing. I do not mean by this that any important changes have been made in the method of performance, but that the audience is perpetually on the look-out for prodigies, and exacts of each that he shall eclipse his forerunners in some phenomenal display of virtuosity.

Never has there been such a run of child-violinists ; yet the public platform is no place for children if they are to have any real child-life and come to natural maturity. It implies such a terribly one-sided development, such a forcing of particular powers and abilities to the certain detriment of others, that if we admit that the emotion excited by these performances is merely an ephemeral amazement, a superficial curiosity, even, in some natures, a kind of jealousy, we must conclude that in no case is the gain worth the sacrifice. The freshness and illimitable hope of childhood are parched and withered by forced contact with reality ; if we leave no blessed leisure for these young imaginings we have done worse than waste, we have cruelly despoiled and slain some few untarnished hours left to an old, sad world.

ON ACCURACY.

THE junior violin teacher, at the start of his career, full of hope and enthusiasm, and not yet acclimatised in his educational environment, often takes for granted that his pupils will turn out reasonably accurate. They achieve so much more exalted things in his roseate visions of the future, that the time and labour which must be spent in laying a firm foundation are unwittingly dwarfed in his mental survey. Gazing upon his dream harvests ripening richly under summer suns he forgets the slow ploughing of winter, till Dame Experience—sharp of tongue and cold of aspect, but not unkind to those that know her—takes him by the scruff of the neck and shows him the wind o' the world whirling his precious seeds over rocks and wantoning waters, and the feet of a multitude treading his darling fields, then bids him labour mightily, and withal be humbly thankful for thin sheaves gathered late and anxiously. But though he cannot shirk this difficult lesson—nor would it be for his truest good to do so—we can, at least, warn him of certain pitfalls by the way, and at the same time adjure him to give more present thought to sowing than to reaping.

Accuracy, alas! is not indigenous to the average pupil. Many and ingenious are his devices for avoiding the beaten track of the normal scale, and the worst of it is that the violin lends itself to all such deviation with deplorable facility.

If the pupil is in doubt as to whether a major or minor third is required, he calmly compromises and gives you an interval which is neither, presently following it up by a leading note of most depressing abasement.   You point out his weaknesses and he tries again, this time giving an opposite rendering but one quite as faulty as the first.   Not even at the fourth and fifth attempt, perhaps, do you get a tolerably correct performance of a simple scale, and the same uncertainty is manifested in his more advanced studies.   Instead of recording a distinct mental photograph of the bar or passage he apparently receives but a blurred impression, and there is a corresponding flaw in his reproduction.

If you are a very junior teacher you, perhaps, give up in despair and let him drift.   His playing doesn't sound so bad to untrained ears, you find; in fact, his people are satisfied with his progress, even think you hard upon him ; and laying this balm to your soul you hope he will awaken in time to a sense of his own deficiencies.

But he will not:—not, at least, unless you keep on striving with him.   Laziness has wonderful staying powers, and it is laziness or constitutional inertia, which prevents him from sufficiently concentrating his mental vision on the particular study.

Of course, apparent laziness may be induced by some physical weakness ; that, you must make it your business to find out.   Teachers sometimes see clearly defects and failings to which familiarity has blinded the parent.   In such cases your duty to the child obliges you to speak ; but with the utmost tact and delicacy.

The most flagrant inaccuracy to which violinists are prone is, naturally, in the matter of intonation.   Where all sounds are evolved directly from the player's consciousness, almost independent of mechanical adjuncts, it stands to reason that unless that consciousness is uniformly critical the sounds will be uncertainly and irregularly produced.   Under responsible guidance the fingers, in due time, become so educated, that they act with what, for want of a better phrase, has been called mechanical precision.   Then, indeed, one might imagine that tiny independent reservoirs of mental energy had begun to develop at the tips.   But this happy condition

does not arrive without a previous period of earnest
and thoughtful labour, and it will never come to the
happy-go-lucky student who has not been trained from
an early stage to criticise his own efforts.

It is because the pupil feels no sense of responsibility
towards his work that he is inaccurate. His attitude
towards disagreeable duties is that of passive endurance
and utter incuriosity. If the teacher can hoist him
up the hill of difficulty, well and good; but he, personally, feels no compelling desire to climb. Very often the
child unconsciously reflects the attitude of the home.
His parents pay the teacher to teach:—let him, then,
teach after his best fashion; inject knowledge by some
patent process of his trade; the need for reciprocity
is entirely uncomprehended.

Such teaching is the dreariest work on earth, and
unfortunately it is a very common experience with the
junior teacher, leading him sometimes to take sombre
views of life according to the quality of his spiritual
fibre. For it is extremely difficult to pierce the triple
wall of ignorance, inertia, and inherited prejudice, and
the sense that his bread is dependent on the success
of the effort is, though stimulating to some natures,
proportionately paralysing to others.

But it is, in this instance, the parents who need to
be taught that it is not sufficient to send a child to
practise for a given time unless some attempt be made to
awaken in him a fitting frame of mind. Otherwise,
he will spend the period to his hurt rather than to his
profit; for every time an inaccuracy is repeated it
approaches more nearly to a habit, and the child who
rarely plays perfectly in tune during the first three
months of his initiation, not really through a defective
sense of pitch but through pure inattention, will seldom
or never arrive at a true sense of what constitutes violin
playing, though he may continue to practise and take
lessons for many unfruitful years.

That is why the junior teacher must be content to
work so slowly and patiently with much of his rough

material. If the pupil is of the temperament that cannot
take pains when the end is not immediately in view, he
is foredoomed to disappointment, and it is better that
he should be discouraged early than after many wasted
hours of superficial study.

But see to it that it is not *you* who are too soon
discouraged. If you give in now under his aggravating
persistency, you are lost ; you will never make anything
of him, and will therefore lose faith in yourself and miss
the legitimate satisfaction that only arises from an
honest day's work.

If we appear to have over-emphasised the evil of
inaccurate intonation it is because it is the first obstacle
in the path of the budding violinist. Supposing it to
have been fairly overcome, there still remains the chance
that he has a weak sense of rhythm, and if so, the
almost certainty that he will abhor counting. Some
little people, again, seem to think that rests of more than
a crotchet's value are wilful waste of time (I well
remember a young lady of nine, saying reproachfully
that to cease for the space of a dotted minim was " just
silly ! ") and steadily ignore them outside of the class-
room. Others affect to perceive no difference between
contrasted styles of bowing. Indeed, the various kinds
and possibilities of inaccuracy are practically numberless ; but they need not be tabulated and attacked as
separate and unrelated foes if once the pupil is personally fired with a desire for thoroughness and a wholesome
contempt for all half-hearted processes. The same spirit
that makes eager conquest of the scale of G will bring
its owner safely through a stiff concerto : hence the
important thing the junior teacher has to teach is not
what but *how* to practise. It is the secret of success,
once gained never lost.

ON SUNDRY ABUSES.

WE may take for granted that the abuse of anything implies that the thing itself is intrinsically
good and desirable, but that it has been unduly
and unwisely employed.

The expression of feeling and sentiment is fitting and
admirable in most music, particularly in that of such
intimately human character as violin music, but excess
of sentiment degenerates easily into sentimentality, and
from that into a sickly and unwholesome emotionalism
which is beneficial neither to player nor public, and
which, indeed, tends to degrade the practice of music to
the level of penny novelette literature, or the pictorial
art of the cigarette box.

There are two classes of violinists who are specially
liable to fall into the gulf of sentimentalism—those who
are by nature impulsive and too easily swayed by the
mood of the moment, and who are keenly susceptible to
the approval of others, and again, those of quite opposite
temperament who have little initiative or judgment, but
who endeavour to model their performances on the lines
of some player who has received the definite cachet of
public approval.

These last succeed, up to a certain point ; imitative
powers are often highly developed in persons of small
intellectual independence ; but the further they are removed from the point of their contact with the original
pattern the more liable they become to miss the spirit
and over-emphasise the letter of some fanciful phrasing

or rhythm. To all so constituted we suggest frequent recourse to the pattern : better still, critical comparison of several patterns (if one may speak of musical performances by so set a term) ; but it is to be feared that such natures have seldom acquired the power of independent criticism, being too prone to accept the popular, even the local verdict, without inquiring too closely into its reasons or values.

This may arise, as we have pointed out elsewhere, either from constitutional inertia, or from false training in early youth, but be the cause what it may the results are much the same. When these violinists have repeated a piece many times with exactly the same nuances and emotional effects it becomes as stale and tedious to the listener's ear as the cheap oleograph of some famous picture is offensive to the educated eye. There is a lack of elasticity, even a sense of insincerity about it which leaves the audience cold and unsatisfied, and contributes its own mite to the wave of nameless depression which is always hovering on the shores of the modern mind.

There is no more dangerous moral influence than the apparent cheapening of a really fine thing. It is more dangerous, because more insidious, than a flagrant violation of the better instincts which, by reason of its very violence, often invokes a salutary recoil ; but the slow deterioration which results from gradual lowering and loss of ideals and delicate appreciations is more truly the " worm i' the bud " that steals strength and beauty from the flower and leaves the man poor in mind and empty of aspiration.

I am not such a fanatic as to say that the occasional indifferent performance of a violin solo leads directly to mental or moral ruin, but I do assert that the frame of mind induced by habitual indifferent performance of music, or of any act whatsoever, and which leads to the uncritical acceptance of the same by a number of slack and devitalised intelligences is, verily, a forcing house of mental and moral disease.

For this reason those violinists of genuinely sympathetic temperament and possessed of more than common insight into the possibilities of music as the refined interpreter of human dreams and desires should sedulously cultivate a power of restraint; *not* that they may move their world less mightily with the magic of the bow, but that they, themselves, be less easily wrought upon by the lower needs and shorter vision of the multitude.

When an artist steps upon the stage he is immediately enveloped in the emanant spirit of the audience; intangible, but none the less powerful. Even as his violin is responsive to atmospheric changes, so is the soul of the violinist responsive to the subtler atmosphere of human thought. As he plays he feels, perhaps, that his listeners are cold ; that he is speaking in a language to which they are unaccustomed and which does not touch them ; then the temptation arises to speak the popular speech; in other words, to play what the man in the street will know and rise to. So for tenderness he gives them the sentimentality of a music hall ballad, and for earnestness mere ranting. The man in the street is noisily pleased. He finds him *bon camarade* ; none of your stiff, high-falutin' fellows that start strange growing-pains in the mind, but just an easy chap like himself, with the addition of a pretty trick of fiddling. The man sitting beside him applauds with the rest, but he is vaguely conscious of disappointment. This music, strange to say, has left his soul poorer instead of richer. But he thinks, perhaps, the fault must be in himself ; he has expected too much . . . but somehow he feels lonely and out of place.

And what of the musician himself—has he no late remorse for the much finer things he might have uttered, and left unsaid ?

No doubt he does feel it at first, but his craving for applause is stronger than his love of art ; besides, applause means money. So he makes sure of his gallery, and always gives what they can easily assimilate.

Putting aside the most important factor, which is, of course, the choice of solos, the methods employed to catch the ear of a certain demonstrative portion of the public are approximately these:—Perpetual tremolo; excessive portamento (often in defiance of the laws of phrasing), deliberate exaggeration of pauses, ritardandos and accelerandos, and a forcing and coarsening of the tone in bravura passages; added to this, occasional peculiarities of stage style and manner which, adopted unconsciously at first, became habitual as soon as they were seen to have attracted public attention.

Needless to say, these are not the great artists; but a child, or immature student who hears such a person spoken of, carelessly, as a "great violinist" is hardly capable of making the distinction between a popular and a really "great" player. He listens, and the exaggerated traits seize him immediately. They are so definite, and so comparatively easy to reproduce. The elements of "greatness" are made plain to him—and vulgarised; for so it is that these abuses of legitimate effects work insidious evil.

It may be a long time before the provincial student hears a truer musician, and meantime he is unconsciously serving a false god—has he not seen the host of his worshippers?—and his artistic aims are proportionately distorted.

Nevertheless we must not forget that it is a living force behind the tawdriness which gives it its dangerous power. The violinist who can touch the heart of any audience is capable of touching them to nobler as well as to baser issues, *but*—and it is a significant small word —he must be their leader, not their slave.

Even the narrowest, dull "man in the street" can be lifted above his perpetual money-strife, or the sordid bliss of the public-house, if only the artist is unselfish in the use of his gift. If the player's aim is purely material success, then will he attract the approval of all like-minded to himself; but if he realises that his power of contributing so largely to the universal beauty in the world is too splendid a thing to be used for merely personal ends, then it is possible for him to become not only a player, but, in some sense, a prophet, quickening souls to keener spiritual life even if they be not of those to whom music usually appeals with special force.

ON VERY SMALL MATTERS.

A ND we will start with the smallest—dirt, pre-
sumably, being composed of an agglomeration of
the minutest particles of "matter in the wrong
place." It is perfectly amazing, the amount of damage
a little dirt can do if it is only allowed to accumulate
quietly. It creeps into the unexplored corners of the
fiddle, under the tailpiece, chin-rest, and fingerboard, and
into the peg-box, not to mention the interior of the
instrument, and settles down over and into the pores of
the wood, checking vibration, and affording food and
shelter to those tiny insects which are not alone harmful
to the fiddle but by no means welcome visitors when they
chance to promenade upon the player's face or neck.

The obvious remedy, though it is not infrequently
overlooked, is, of course, to keep a clean, soft rag—
preferably an old silk or linen handkerchief—always
ready in one pocket of the case, by means of which
the exterior dirt, at all events, can be carefully removed.
But this operation, simple as it seems, is not one to
be entrusted to careless hands, as manipulation just
a shade too rough might be attended with awkward
consequences.

Resin should never be allowed to accumulate about the
feet of the bridge. The majority of little players have
grasped this demonstrable fact, but many of them forget
to track the finer dust of it into the out-of-sight corners,
where it is just waiting for the first damp day or over-
heated room to turn abominably sticky. Again, resin,
while in use, should not be held in the naked fingers.

K

Not only does it come off upon the fingers but their moisture adheres to it, and prevents it from running freely on the hair. I have seen much resin spoiled in this way.

Besides, the hands may not be quite clean. The "powers that be" may have insisted upon vigorous employment of soap and water before the small person left home; but many curious and interesting things have been examined *en route* and have left indisputable traces.

Well, these traces must be removed, otherwise the strings will become both false and unsightly; and there is nothing in the violin world more objectionable than a frayed and dirty string, thick and uncertain of speech and whistling at every second note. E string, fortunately in this case, breaks in due course; A and D continue to a disreputable old age; but it is far better that they should be removed than allowed to remain on the violin when they are obviously unfit for melodious use.

Returning to the subject of resin: I have a strong preference for the kind known as "Hidersine," both because it is usually of good substance, and also because of the fact that it is attached to a small piece of non-absorbent material which keeps it from contact with the fingers, preserves it from passing impurities, and permits it to be conveniently used down to the last scrap. It is a little more expensive than the customary cake in a cardboard case (with which it commonly parts company during the first week), but it outlasts several specimens of this variety, while the undetachable wrapping renders it invaluable in the junior classes.

Another important accessory which often suffers from neglect is the bow hair. It is, naturally, affected by dirty strings or bad resin, but it sometimes happens that it is spoiled either by too much or an insufficient application of resin.

If the surface of the hair has a shiny or glistening appearance under the light, then it needs more resin than it has been getting, but if the powder flies off in clouds, or has actually become clogged or gritty on the part nearest the nut, it may be necessary to wash the hair before it can be brought into proper condition. If, in addition to greasiness, the supply of hair be worn thin, it is better to have the bow re-haired at once; but if cleansing is all that is necessary, proceed as follows:—

Remove the screw at the nut and loosen the hair, taking care to prevent it from twisting. Have ready a soapy lather, about the heat and consistency required for washing woollens, and immerse the hair, passing it gently backwards and forwards through the fingers till it feels thoroughly cleansed. On no account allow it to become tangled, or the screw attachment to get wet. Rinse in several waters and shake out loose moisture. Dry at a little distance from a clear fire. When perfectly dry, insert screw and tighten. Scrape a little resin, very fine, on a sheet of notepaper and rub in; then the bow is ready for use. Whenever a hair breaks, cut off the broken lengths; never pull them out, as doing so invariably loosens others.

When putting on a new set of strings, see that each coil keeps, approximately, to its own side of the peg-box, and never coil a greater length of gut round the peg then is actually necessary to secure it. Beware, also, that thicker strings, the third in particular, are not wound in such a manner, with one coil crossing another, as to be specially liable to slip under the pressure of playing and cause a sudden lowering of pitch most disconcerting to the inexperienced player.

Another slip which sometimes occurs is, sad to relate, in the matter of temper. Few of us but are more or less subject to climatic influences, and when, in addition to unkind skies, the appurtenances of our trade seem possessed by an imp of contrariety and distract us with all imaginable shortcomings and perversities, the advent of a reluctant small child, suffering under much the same evil combination of circumstances, is apt to add fuel to smouldering flame. Something is to blame, somewhere, and we cannot come to grips with it; but that something is *not* the child, himself a victim, who bears our onslaught in dumb and impotent revolt. That we shall be sorry afterwards is no preventive at the time, and yet—how sorry we are! But if we could only realise that the child is in reality a fellow sufferer, with added disabilities, we might, as it were, take ourselves by the shoulders at the start, lay violent hands upon an innocent joke or two, and so doing, change the dangerous current of affairs.

Unpunctuality is another fruitful source of trouble. The few minutes late at the beginning of a busy day will sometimes have piled themselves into a harassing hour by evening, even to the extent of making the teacher feel that he has just tipped the balance at over-work. Then, again, the pupil who is late and breathless, or late and smilingly unconcerned—which is too often the way of young ladies of leisure—is hardly in a frame of mind to get the best value out of the lesson ; besides which, if there are other students awaiting their turn, some portion of the culprit's work must be left out in order to accommodate the more virtuous. It is invariably difficult to teach the value of time to persons who, having no regular or responsible occupations, are usually much too busy about doing nothing in particular to achieve anything with thoroughness, or at a definite hour.

VIOLINISTS—SOLO AND ORCHESTRAL.

IT is all very well to say that an ideal leader of orchestra—like a leader of armies—is born, not made: this is one of those truisms which, by its very finality, is apt to blind one to the component parts of its evolution. The distinctive qualities of a leader, like those of a conductor, a *première danseuse*, or an orator, must, certainly, be inherent; but they will not come to fruit unless they are fed and nourished by education and experience.

The ground work of the musical education of a solo violinist and an orchestral player is the same. Up to a certain point in student life they not only study alike, technical and artistic studies and pieces, but apparently profit alike from the same material. Then, following the lines of growth of mind and character, there comes a time when they begin to differentiate; to show preferences: to have already different aims, different horizons. The soloist becomes more and more concerned with the perfection of detail; with his personal attitude towards music in general and his chosen solos in particular. Music exists for him, at this time, first, as a means of intimate and refined self-expression, and in a lesser degree, of interpreting the thought and feeling of others. Even where he consciously subordinates his ego to such a master as Bach, Beethoven, or Brahms, he is, nevertheless, all the while as it were, taking him by the hand and saying to his audience, " See what friends we are, this fellow and I ! How perfectly we

understand one another!"—and this in no dictatorial
or impertinent spirit, but as the natural outcome of
his real talents and training.

The orchestral player, proper, has not, perhaps, the
same delicate quality of insight and sympathy in his
rendering of solo parts, nor does he feel the same im-
perative need for individual expression. His attitude
towards music is more impersonal. He conceives of
it as a whole, in which he is consciously a part, and
his rôle is rather that of the devoted disciple than the
master. His happiness lies in intelligent acquiescence ;
he wishes to be incorporated in the artistic unity as
a devout Buddhist in Nirvana.

You may say, perhaps, that this is extravagant ; that
it is an exaggeration of the temperamental differences,
innate, but difficult of definition, which characterize the
ideal soloist and the ideal " first fiddle " : but as it is
sometimes necessary to emphasize certain colourings in
order that the picture may speak more clearly to the
eye, so, in this case, it is necessary to accentuate the
lines of divergence precisely because it is on account
of non-comprehension of such temperamental differences
that amateur musicians sometimes find themselves in
the very uncomfortable position of square pegs in round
holes.

A case illustrative of this came under my notice only
the other day. The inhabitants of a certain wealthy
quarter of a provincial city, which happened to be rather
rich in musical material, were desirous of getting up
a small orchestra of fifteen or twenty performers, under
a professional conductor, which should be available for a
forthcoming festival. A lady, who was the particular
star of local concerts, was almost unanimously chosen as
leader, and the practices commenced. But, from an
early stage, one or two experienced players were sensible
of an indefinable constraint and uncertainty which
presently permeated the whole band. The fact became
clear that the lady leader, while possessing undeniable
artistic and technical ability, was lacking in just that

solidity, responsibility, and discrimination which are requisite to a good leader. Neither conductor nor comrades felt sure of her, and but for the presence, at the second desk, of a less brilliant, but more reliable player, the performances might have been attended with disaster. As it was, the lady of whom so much had been expected felt troubled and, perhaps, slighted ; but did not in the least realize that she was disqualified for the post in spite of, and indeed by reason of, the qualities of her particular gifts. As well might one expect support and substance from a willow or a climbing rose as steady grip and vigour from such an ultra-sensitive and emotionally variable temperament.

Do not infer that the leading violinist of the orchestra need not, or must not possess musical intuition and an emotional nature; on the contrary, he will never respond to his conductor, or carry his fellows with him, unless he has both sympathy and spirit. But they must be subservient to his sense of duty and not narrowed. to the merely personal point of view.

The distinguishing mark of the casual, who will never be a real orchestral player, is his or her distaste for subordinate and inner parts. "Give me the tune?" they cry; and, granted a good leader, they will often follow the tune very well, and even take the trouble to practise the more difficult passages. But set them, for the good of their souls, to a second fiddle part, or the accompaniment to a recitative, and there is a lamentable falling off:—dismay and upbraiding, and sometimes, even a disgusted exit from the orchestra. They have no real taste for it, and are just as well out of the way. At the opposite pole, the person who takes instinctively to viola parts has usually all the orchestral qualities in a nutshell. He sits, as it were, in the centre of the chord, linking high and low and mellowing all by the sober richness of his tones, whilst round about him is woven, circling ever outward, the widening web of harmony. Comparatively few viola players, I imagine, ever take kindly to any other instrument : it, and its place in the whole of string concerted music, exercise a peculiar fascination over its chosen votaries.

To return to our violin student : he, while he is still uncertain of his particular gifts and capacities—though most of us, after all, are of average, all-round capacity, capable of being trained to average proficiency in either direction, but possibly to distinction in neither—should receive steady and progressive training in concerted as well as solo music, for, after all, the bulk of the orchestra is made up of just such players, who are neither distinctively of one class nor the other, but who, nevertheless, do excellent work in their several places in the band, and also contrive to extract a very considerable amount of enjoyment out of their services.

ON MUSICAL EXAMINATIONS.

ON the subject of musical examinations there is, of course, considerable diversity of opinion. Some professors of the violin have a strong objection to them; based, perhaps, on the idea that they tend too much to the development of merely technical and mechanical ability as compared with artistic. Others, on the contrary, are so much impressed with the value of these educational tests that they practically specialize in this direction.

That the majority of parents and guardians are similarly impressed is borne practical witness to by the prevalence and success of such professional advertisements as include the magic words, "prepares for all examinations," in their formula.

Admittedly, examinations are a reputable test of both pupils and teachers, and parents and guardians who are not personally capable of measuring the pupil's progress do well to assure themselves that it exists by means of such periodical trials. But, as with every other question, there is something to be said on both sides. We will take the pros first.

Preparation for the musical examinations held by those schools and colleges of the highest standing, if undertaken in an understanding spirit, ensures, firstly, regularity in the daily violin practice; secondly, a judicious apportionment of the time so spent; thirdly, more scrupulous attention to accuracy, in all aspects, than might otherwise have been given.

It rests with the teacher to impress upon the elder the necessity of this regular practising, not only because of the general improvement in playing to which it contributes, but in relation to the second matter, judicious apportionment of time. If irregular practising is the rule, the most uncongenial subject, viz., scales, technical exercises, or studies, will be sure to come off with scant attention ; being put off from day to day till a more favourable opportunity.

Such a method of study is quite worthless in regard to preparing for examinations ; and by impressing this very definitely on the responsible persons, the teacher may succeed in getting more and better quality of work from the pupil than he would do if there were no particular aim in view.

This touches, also, the matter of accuracy. Violin playing which, hitherto, had passed for tolerable, or even very good, in the family circle, if declared by a teacher of approved judgment to be not up to examination standard, will be more critically appreciated in future. The listeners may not be able to judge of peculiar technical faults, but they will seize on general deficiencies, and learn to watch for improvement in particular directions to which their attention may have been called.

With the average run of easy-going, averagely-gifted children, the mental, moral and technical discipline necessarily undergone in course of preparing for even the earliest violin examinations is of very great benefit, especially to those who are suffering—as is so often the case nowadays—from over-indulgent and inconsistent home training. The habit of expecting children to "grow" good, and systematically refraining from even the mildest coercive methods during childhood, is responsible for much of the ill-health, undeveloped moral instincts, and general unpreparedness to battle with the world which characterises the children of a certain class of fairly well-to-do people to-day.

Discipline and training in Nature—the shaping of all animate things to a definite end ; deliberate self-sacrifice, even among creatures accounted low in the scale of creation—is traceable throughout all ages, and in the history of every branch of animal life. Is it reasonable, then, to expect that man, a creature of exceptional powers and capacities, will set his qualities to the best possible uses in life without that preliminary discipline and training in obedience to universal laws which even a cat gives to her kitten or a sparrow to her young?

But even in so small a matter as an early violin examination the teacher has it in his (or, more often, in *her*) power to counteract, to some extent, this unfortunate atmosphere of irresolution and indecision. All the same, it is neither an easy nor, often, a grateful task, to instil into uncurbed human nature the rudimentary notions of obedience and concentration. Yet, it is a noticeable thing that children often grow more attached to those who are comparatively stern with them than to those who are indulgent but unstable. It is a natural instinct, that of reliance on strength and justness, which is awakened; and no teacher of the violin need fear losing the affection of her pupils if she gives credit where credit is due, and enforces her will wisely and quietly, by the methods which are best adapted to the characteristics of the particular child.

This, as I have said, is the favourable side of the question; let us now turn to the other.

There is a certain danger of formalism which insidiously attacks those who are in the habit of preparing pupils, year after year, for the same round of examinations, and who are so thoroughly well up in their work that they have acquired the reputation of being "crack" coaches in their own peculiar line. The danger lies for them, to some extent, in an attempt (perhaps unconscious) to force all growing student nature into that one definite mould which has acquired an accepted value in the eyes of the musical world. With the majority of children, no doubt, the method is attended with quite desirable consequences; but, in some few cases, it may result in the abortion or starvation of attributes and tendencies which had, at first, inherent possibilities of excellence.

This is specially liable to occur if too little latitude is allowed in the matter of musical interpretation, which is a thing intimately coloured and influenced by the personal characteristics of the performer, and in which independent judgment often shows itself at a comparatively early age in students of more than average artistic feeling. But it not infrequently occurs that these imaginative students are of a highly-strung and delicate nervous organisation, and have a difficulty in sustaining the physical efficiency requisite to the task.

Under these circumstances, I do not think that examinations are always desirable, not so much because of the routine of preparation as because of the nervous excitement aroused by the actual event, and the occasional overstrain of the last weeks' practising.

This is especially applicable to girl students of from twelve to fifteen years of age, or older, who are keenly anxious to do well, but whose intelligence is, perhaps, in advance of their technical capacity.

The violin is, of all instruments, the most difficult to manipulate under adverse conditions of body and mind, and the result of a bad failure is sometimes so discouraging that it has a long and anything-but-useful effect on the unfortunate candidate. Nevertheless, in cases when examinational tests are enforced by parents or guardians on highly nervous candidates, these disadvantageous conditions can be somewhat mitigated by tactful management and watchful care on the part of the teacher.

THE FORMATION OF MUSICAL STYLE.

PERHAPS there is hardly any period in the provincial violin student's career which is fraught with such danger to his ultimate progress as that during which, having arrived at some technical proficiency, he is supposed to be forming his musical style. (The word "provincial" is here used to denote more limited educational possibilities than fall to the lot of the student in the greater schools and more cosmopolitan cities). Only too often he forms it purely parrot-wise, by unintelligent imitation of the manner or mannerisms of his betters. Even if those betters be of the very best, the mere act of copying their performances helps not at all to develop his own understanding, and his repertoire is necessarily limited to those pieces which he imagines himself to reproduce with most faithful exactitude.

Equally undesirable with this is too rigid adherence to the tenets of any particular violin school, or system of technique. Doubtless, the violinist who originated the school or system was in a very safe and healthy condition of mind because he was obligatorily progressive. But, as schools and systems become set, rounded off and tabulated; as they pass through the usual stages, from the intelligent development of the originator to the passive reflection of the imitator, they grow more formal and inelastic. The suggestions of the pioneer crystallize into the dogma of the disciple, and the informing spirit gradually deserts the husk, leaving what sometimes proves to be an obstacle in the path instead of an aid to progress. This refers to the abuse of any system, not to the discriminating use of it; for it does not follow that the whole scheme is worthless because the information on special subjects is out of date or insufficient. There may be a gold mine in an arid waste, and the prospector needs, before all things, a discerning spirit, and the exercise of impartial criticism in sifting true ore from rubbish. If the student becomes in his turn a teacher of the violin, it is even more necessary that he, lest he lead others astray, should select his teaching formulas with care, and from a wide field.

What is true of the older schools is applicable also to the modern. One method turns out a very perfect machine—but the soul is lacking. Another brings some special technical detail to an unprecedented measure of perfection, but leaves others of equal importance untouched. A third is in the highest degree intellectual and thought-compelling, but fails to be of practical use unless supplemented by some purely mechanical training. They are excellent, each in its particular aspect; but no one of them, alone, affords everything the student requires, nor can supply him with an adequate, all-round musical training.

Then, again, for this fashion of going to hear one famous artist play Paganini, or Wieniawski; and another, Bach, Beethoven, or Mendelssohn, and subsequently furnishing a feeble and colourless replica of some characteristic expositions, with the statement that you have modelled your style upon that of So-and-so! Well, it is about as satisfactory as the copy of a court dress by a village dressmaker.

For one thing, it doesn't fit. There is almost always some delicacy of phrasing or bowing, some subtle variation of tone or nicety of rhythmical balance that you have just missed, or misunderstood, and for lack of which the thing is spiritually dead. Or, possibly, you may have grasped the artist's intention, but exaggerate his suggestive manner of conveying it. And, in either case, a pianola or a gramophone would give as much or more pleasure. Moreover, it is no real "style" that you have acquired; you are merely masquerading in an ill-fitting and awkward adaptation of other men's mental garments.

Go to hear these virtuosi, by all means; hear them and compare them, and let the hearing and comparison sink in. And when you have let the results simmer for a while, go to your violin and see whether the composer says anything directly to you; or whether what he has spoken through the fingers of these others is, indeed, the last word you are capable of receiving on the subject. But whatever you do, don't imitate blindly and unconvincingly.

The formation of a musical style (in reality the expression of personality) proceeds mainly by fearless analysis of all knowledge life brings to your ken, and by thoughtful application of the same to the mind and mood of the composer as embodied in his work: also, by adaptation of the natural and acquired forces at your command to the interpretation of a clearly-conceived artistic whole. You must be perfectly at home with the idea before you can impress it on others. Mere imitators fail by lack of inward certainty, and by reason of a certain bluntness of perception which seizes the rough outline, but misses the perspective.

To some the understanding spirit comes by birthright, an exquisite and wonderful gift; to others, again, it is the fruit of the years' experience, the late blossom of toil. But to him who has the listening ear, the just and enquiring mind, it *will* come, at some time and in some fashion.

Perception, comparison, and selection, these are our working tools, and the workshop is the world. Perception says to the soul "Awake! Here is something fresh, something fine! Do you not feel how this man makes the heart throb and the blood leap with the enkindling spirit of his style! Does he not dazzle us with his brilliancy, amaze us with his certainty?"

" Aye," say Comparison, " but do you remember how, some little while ago, another played to us this very theme? Was there not, perhaps, in his music something less clamant, less assured, but more spiritual, more inspiring; something that drew all humanity a little closer, and fluttered for a moment the veil of the Unseen?"

" It is true," rejoins Selection, " but we owe honour to them both. And we would marry this man's martial ardour with the white flame of that other soul; would bulwark tenderness with virile force, and of the ideal union evoke a more consummate art. It may be that our members are unequal to the task, that we are handicapped by physical defects or faults of character, but, at least, we are vouchsafed clear vision of our goal, and strive thereto with steadfast eyes and eager will."

By such methods—less fanciful, no doubt, but similar in essence—shall we alone arrive at a true, vivid, and harmonious expression of ourselves and of that musical art which it is given to us to interpret.

Underlying all music is the soul of the universe; the life and love of man, the brief day of a flower, the chisel of time at work on immemorial rocks. If this great pulse beats all unheard by you, unguessed at even, as you pile up note on note, cadence on cadence, scale on chord, the whole as devoid of meaning and consistency as a child's castle in the sand, you are no artist; you have missed the reason of it all, have taken tinsel for true gold, and starved your soul before a teeming harvest.

There is no joy in copying: it is a task, unfruitful, hopeless. Out of the chaos of notes let there come to the soul, as dawn to the earth, first, a flush in the greyness and a tremor of waking life, then, the sun in his glory, and a new day born for you. Let music include and be included in the whole; not kept as an ornament for Sabbaths and feast-days, too fine and much too foreign to the common, wholesome week. Music that does not spring from natural feeling provokes an artificial atmosphere, a poor, thin air, most difficult to breathe in ; it is a thing useless alike to listener and performer.

Remember, then, if you are tempted to acquire a "style" by other than the natural means, that you will merely overlay intelligence with the débris of other minds, and choke the channels whereby nature lends to inarticulate things a passing voice.

ON OPPORTUNITIES.

TO every one of us, fiddlers, factors, or financiers, there has surely come, in the days of our novitiate, at least one door of opportunity standing ajar upon an unknown country, and it may be that the tenor of subsequent years has been decided by whether we passed through boldly, or halted waveringly upon the threshold till the latch clicked and the key turned. We, passing onward, half sad and half respited, said, perhaps, "To-morrow it may be open again; and then, indeed, we will no longer hesitate, but step out firmly on the untried path, and scan the fresh horizon and the opening view." But, alas! opportunity has no morrow. Upon the road of life there is no standing still nor yet returning; and the same threshold never echoes twice to the same feet. Some distant chink may open on a new campaign; some future opportunity invite us to press on, and out of the old rut, but never *that* closed door, that shining chance that we have missed—let slip.

To all musicians, and especially to professional violinists, it is supremely necessary to grasp every opportunity of wider interests, of unprofessional knowledge. Specialization, too rigidly pursued, is apt to narrow character. It runs like a paved alley, between shadowing walls, with here, perhaps, a hint of blossomy sweetness in the wingless air, and there a sound of unseen waters, but cloistered from the varied press of life and thought. A man's but half a man who owns no interests but in one direction, and it will not take from, but increase the violinist's peculiar skill if he be also some-

thing of a painter, a poet, or a naturalist.   His playing
may perhaps lack somewhat of that extreme agility
which exacts unceasing servitude, but even that I doubt
—or, perhaps, I undervalue—and he will gain immensely
in freshness, firmness and elasticity.

Modern professional life, for the many who are not
highly gifted, but who are nevertheless conscientious,
earnest and diligent violinists, is a perpetual struggle to
keep pace in the ranks.   At certain seasons this struggle
becomes so intense that there are no hours spared from
the actual musical preoccupation save those that are
necessarily devoted to sleep.   This is existence in a
state of slavery, not worthy to be called life ; and yet it
is passed in the service of art!—a thing which must
be fed with beauty !   Let me make it plain that this is
not the voluntary service offered up by the devotee,
which finds rich reward for physical toil and mental
striving in the knowledge gained thereby, and which has
no need to assume to the world more surety than it feels,
nor direct its efforts to any poor temporary expediency.
No, this is a sordid affair of merely keeping place :—
keeping pupils, in plain words, or some post which is
really, though not nominally, competitive.   To this work,
complicated perhaps by domestic anxieties, the violinist
brings, day after day, a tired mind and body, and finds,
perhaps, that he is just able to keep abreast—a little
falling back in intonation, or a momentary slackening of
nerve is such a dangerous thing!—just able to hold his
head above the next man who is pressing up the ladder.
Of course competition is equally keen in the great centres
in respect of almost any form of professional labour, but
the musician's attitude towards his particular métier is
popularly supposed to be different from that of a
solicitor, a stockbroker, or a merchant towards his ;
while, nevertheless, the conditions under which the
musician works are usually quite as commercial as, if
anything, more depressingly so, those of the recognised
men of business.   The thing to wonder at and be thankful for is, rather, that so much refinement and artistic

sense survive in the average hard-worked teacher or
bandsman than that he does not become an utter
automaton, or an audacious charlatan.

But there is usually one comparatively slack period in
the violinist's year, determined by the character of the
work he is engaged on, and that is his chance to pursue
his second study, or any hobby of a sufficiently intellectual kind to afford him matter for congenial thought
during the few spare moments of the busy time. The
word intellectual is not here to be construed in any
pedantic sense; it merely indicates recreation which
affords mental exercise and refreshment as distinct from
that which is purely physical, such as football or golf,
which, though no doubt excellent in present action,
are of little value in lengthened retrospect. Discriminating reading in one or more languages, the study of a
special branch of natural science (or several branches)
experimental interests in chemistry, in botany, in
sociology, in political economy, in painting, in *anything*
that stores the mind with food against the day of
drought is a weapon wherewith to fight the demons
of discouragement and fatigue.

Matthew Arnold, in one of his " Essays in Criticism,"
suggests the use of certain lines of poetry of recognised
and undeniable beauty as touchstones for those whose
claim to beauty is yet unproven. Any objects or ideas
which call up the most exalted feelings which the mind
is capable of may be considered as such touchstones,
and if mentally resorted to will have the effect of keeping
alive ideals and resolutions which might otherwise
perish for lack of nourishment. The remembrance of
sombre crests against a sunset sky;—of whispering
waters' under harvest moons;—of splendid words that
winged a noble thought;—of deeds that moved the
world, and loves that beacon down the centuries with
undying flame;—these, the immortally beautiful, alone
can keep the mean and sordid from eating up his life
with ever-hungry cares and fears. The danger of lowering his standard to what "pays," and to what is under-

stood by the half-educated portion of the public as success in life, is averted by keeping steadfast eyes upon the truly beautiful (not necessarily as expressed in music, for beauty is catholic, and the essence of it is the same in all manifestations), and though the importunate facts of paying the butcher and the baker, and the keeping up of appearances which is the inevitable lot of the struggling professional man, remain, and levy their exacting demands on the greater part of the violinist's time and intelligence, there will still be a haven where they cannot enter, and a refuge from the nagging tongue of expediency.

ON WEAK SIGHT AND HEARING.

THERE are quite a number of people who would meet with indignant denial the statement that they were just a little deaf, or rather inconveniently shortsighted, but who, nevertheless, if they were to take up the study of the violin, would find out fast enough that they were indeed, in more or less degree, hampered by these deficiencies.

If it is a case of simple short sight, it can easily be assisted by the aid of suitable glasses; but there is a variety of defective sight which is known as astigmatism which requires more specialized treatment, and which sometimes misleads the sufferer because it is not always exactly "short," but manifests itself in an uncomprehended difficulty of focus, much local strain and weariness, and frequently by headache; which last is seldom put down to the right cause. Musical type is even more trying than ordinary printed characters to sight of this kind, because of its irregularity in outline and the necessity for extremely rapid visualization as well as accuracy. The visual nerves as well as the mental perceptions of players in orchestral or chamber music are subjected to a severe strain; one, which, if not alleviated by every mechanical means, is apt to result in serious deterioration of health. As in the case of short sight, the first thing to do is to consult an oculist; subsequently, to select an optician who can be depended on to make such alterations in the position of the glasses as may periodically be found necessary, without further advice from the oculist. The headache and weariness may not pass away all at once; it often takes some little time to get used to the glasses and to rest the strained nerves.

Another thing about which violinists should be as particular as possible is the quality and position of artificial light. Of course, in the orchestra, or on many occasions of concerted playing, it stands to reason that not all performers can have equally comfortable positions with regard to the light, and the earnest amateur or junior professional is not recommended to make himself a nuisance to his conductor and fellow members in order to obtain for himself the greatest possible illumination. But he is entitled, in reason, to secure for himself and his comrades the best available accommodation in this respect, even if it means a little additional outlay on the part of the director or company under which he serves. Conductors and secretaries of many amateur musical societies are sometimes so much above mere details, and so much more taken up with artistic effects, that they overlook mere convenience, which would, none the less, contribute largely to the real achievement of success.

Geniuses can apparently make bricks without straw, but the average workman turns out better work accordingly as he has efficient tools and a comfortable workshop. The workshop, as regards the pit of a provincial theatre or music hall, or the practising room of a small municipal or working men's band is very commonly ill-ventilated, ill-lighted, and in other respects unsuitable. Enthusiasm can overlook a great deal of discomfort and inconvenience in a beloved cause; but there is, in many cases, no reason why it should be called upon to do this, or why the work or play should be carried on under conditions detrimental to particular organs, or to the general health. Improvements in these matters might be set on foot by the players themselves, with the expenditure of some thought, and by tactful representation at headquarters.

Concerning private practising, the violinist or 'cellist has only himself to blame if he neglects to use all possible precautions not to overstrain his weak sight. In the first place, he must so place himself that the light shall fall from behind him on the page, preferably

over the left shoulder. Checkered sunlight, which out-
lines the pattern of a curtain, or some prominent object
partially on the page is decidedly to be avoided; so,
also, is flickering gas, or any artificial light of unsteady
flame. A standard lamp of the " Belge " type is one of
the best lights I know of for the violinist's purpose,
provided good oil be used. If the glare of sunlight on
the white sheet is felt to be too strong (particularly if
playing out-of-doors), slightly darkened glasses may be
found useful; but these as a rule, should not be worn
without medical advice. (The use of dark glasses has a
very depressing effect on persons of anæmic habit, who
are predisposed to despondency). Cold-water bandages,
worn at night, are also a great relief to tired eyes; but
these as well as the dark glasses should not be tried
without advice, or unless the violinist is quite sure that
there is no other eye-trouble except ordinary fatigue.

With regard to deafness :—It is quite possible for the
ear to be ordinarily responsive to all ordinary sounds,
including conversation, and yet to be slightly obtuse, or
at least very easily confused where the violin or kindred
instruments is concerned. That is not what is known
musically as a " bad " ear, though no doubt it is allied to
it; it simply means that the student has a difficulty,
perhaps, in tuning in the orchestra; in distinguishing
which note of two is faulty in double stopping; or that
after prolonged practice of difficult passages on the
higher third of the fingerboard, he is less certain at the
end than at the beginning of the relative pitch of his
intervals. Notes of extreme pitch, either high or low,
lose for him their characteristic musical flavour sooner—
that is, at a less extreme pitch—than for others; and,
uncomfortably conscious of something lacking, he strives
to impress tonality by sheer reiteration. But it is
beating the air. If he were to play the passage two or
three times at the beginning of the day—when his ear is
fresh and unwearied and less likely to be confused by
the strain put upon it in its weakest capacity—he would
have some chance of getting it right eventually; but the

perpetual repetition of sounds which are almost outside his natural perception, outrage the aural nerves and cause them to revolt by a condition of tone deafness, which will extend, if the student persists in the ordinary method of practising, over a much larger area of the fingerboard. This species of deafness is allied to what is called " throat deafness," and varies very much with the general condition of health. The anxiety of preparing for an examination is very apt to bring it on even where it has not already been known to exist ; and in that case the student is strongly advised to let the examination alone for a year, or a half-year, as he will certainly be unable to do himself justice under the specially trying circumstances. Rest and a nerve tonic, and, in aggravated cases, the advice of a specialist, are usually necessary before the ear returns to its normal condition. But I do not believe that a person suffering from this kind of deafness—even though it is almost imperceptible in relation to anything else but some passages and combinations of music—can ever conquer it sufficiently, or train it, as may sometimes be done in cases of ordinary "bad" ear, if it is not too bad, to become a professional violinist with any degree of satisfaction in or reliance on himself. He would probably be much more successful with some other class of instrument less susceptible to variation of tonality. Amateur violinists, on the other hand, if they avoid passages or compositions which strain the ear, may continue to play and often give a great deal of pleasure to their friends if they are musically gifted. But in this case also, reiteration of a phrase which is liable to be played out of tune is not to be recommended for more than a comparatively few repetitions. The finger work may be practised soundlessly if mere rapidity of fingering is required, but under no circumstances will it pay to fatigue a delicate ear ; and, after all, the amateur is not bound, like the professional, to attain any very great degree of technical proficiency, and he can also choose his music in accordance with his natural abilities.

ON CHARACTERISTICS OF THE
VIOLIN.

THOSE to whom the characteristic quality of violin music—or more truly, violin voice—most strongly appeals are usually those in whose temperament there is an underlying strain of melancholy, and a hunger after things at present unattainable. They are by no means despondent or devitalized people, but are none the less inwardly unsatisfied with life as it is; they yearn for a fuller, finer and freer expression of human possibilities, and something in the tones of a violin—especially one which has been fashioned by a master's hand—affords a natural voice and solace to this otherwise unexpressed desire.

> '' Who comes, to-day, with sunlight on his face,
>   And eyes of fire, that have a sorrow's trace,
>   But are not sad with sadness of the years,
>   Or hints of tears?
>
> See how he bends to greet his soul's desire
>   His violin, which trembles like a lyre,
>   And seems to trust him, and to know his touch,
>   Belov'd so much ! ''
>
> (*Pablo de Sarasate*, E. MACKAY).

Most instruments of other species are comparatively bound and fettered by their more mechanical conditions of utterance, which, while rendering them infinitely safer company for the person of limited gift and ability,

detract proportionately from their possibilities of pleasure
for those more richly dowered. The piano and organ
are to some, and in some ways, more satisfying instruments because of their straightforwardness and the almost
unlimited scope they afford for harmonic combination.
But they are only satisfying because they never touch
the illimitable and unattainable. They compass that
which can be perfectly compassed, weighed, measured
and dissected; they render with admirable fidelity the
form and substance of certain music; but they are
unalterably orthodox (not after Chesterton). They are,
as it were, the great Middle Class of music, sound,
solidly excellent and praiseworthy, following, indeed,
upon the antics of the fiddle with a timorous and halting
tread as after one who, be he vagabond or noble, cock o'
the walk at village feast or priest at the high altar, is,
at best or worst, a conscienceless fellow of whom one
can predict nothing certainly, but who yet has qualities
that command respect – nay, even a floodtide of enthusiasm, which most excellent piano and organ can never
quite attain to, toil they never so well and wisely. They
are musical instruments; but a fiddle is something more.

A fiddle in the hands of a true fiddler is no affair
of wood and gut, but something vibrant, keen, and
quick; the home of spirits, of—one knows not what?
—of forest memories, of the soul of him who made it,
gave it voice and individuality, saturated it, maybe, with
his thought and travail; of the many who have touched
and played it, ill or well, and whose life-story has been
told in solitary hours to this one faithful confidant;
whose hopes have made it joyous as a mated lark in
May, whose sorrows, sad as winds that sigh about an
empty home.

So near has it been to life, it almost lives. And
surely, if the empty room wherein some finely-tempered
spirit has toiled, thought, and suffered through many
long and difficult days, and slowly wrought that toil and
suffering into forms of strength and beauty, can hold—
as some folks deem it can—for kindred spirits a presence

that is more than memory—some secret brooding on the brink of life, that stirs the folded curtain of the night; how little need we wonder then that a violin—a thing so near, so intimate, and dependent on the hand that touches it—should keep some spiritual fragrance of the souls it knew.

But this is for the few, not for the crowd. Yet many a lover finds, perhaps, more eloquent utterance in his music than his halting tongue can compass. Many an eager soul, tethered to a treadmill of small duties endlessly performed for life's small change, finds in a humble violin a voice from other worlds, breathing of peace, and wider skies and loveliness—a single outlet for his soul's desire.

Great as is the number and famous as are many of the sonatas written as duets for violin and piano, a more incompatible couple, as a matter of fact, cannot well be imagined. Not even Beethoven could wed the two with any profound and natural harmony. Like many similar human couples, they have become adjusted to, and tolerant of each other after years of enforced companionship, but fundamental unity there is none. And the piano has improved and developed along lines which separate it still further from its more mercurial yoke-fellow. The piano in its youth—the old-fashioned spinet or harpsichord—though in itself a much poorer thing, was not isolated in its own perfections. Like many a modern woman who has looked life in the face and deliberately taken up her place therein, neither yielding to, nor receiving service from man's mind, but deeming her own completely furnished for her needs, the modern piano is complete within itself, neither yielding to, nor receiving companionship from any other instrument except, perhaps, the human voice. Violin and piano present the spectacle of a creature of limited but impeccable excellence wedded to one of visible imperfections, but who is gifted with the poet's eye, the poet's heart: they walk together, but are yet incommunicably apart.

One has only to listen to the "Kreutzer" Sonata, played by a couple of artists, to recognise this in its fulness—that is, if one comes to it with unprejudiced mind. It is not a duet; it is an association of two instruments by force of will, not sympathy. If it happens to be followed by a string trio or quartet one is immediately struck by the difference. In this one finds true harmony, perfect compatibility.

If it were possible to improve and develop the guitar to such an extent as to greatly facilitate the execution of rapid passages, to increase its sustaining power, to extend its range and equalise and intensify its tonal capacity, it already possesses natural qualities which render it a suitable comrade to a fiddle. Perhaps no instrument of any pretentions to dignity and worth has suffered more at the hands of ignorant and incompetent performers than the guitar; but if there could be found a master-craftsman willing to devote himself to the development and perfecting of this instrument, I am persuaded that it would yet take rank with those of the most widely recognised merit.

There is a round sweetness and fulness about the tone of a good Lacote or Panormo guitar which—if it could be preserved without deterioration, with the addition to the mechanism of the instrument of many modern improvements and adjustments such as might suggest themselves to one skilled in such matters—is worthy to be redeemed from the oblivion into which it is undoubtedly falling owing to various deterrent minor causes.

ON MAKING A CONNEXION.

THE first serious consideration for every violin student who has taken out his or her final diploma, with a view to making professional use of it, is, naturally, how to establish a connexion. The means which may be chosen to this end are of course affected by the intention and capacity of the individual to pursue his avocation as performer or teacher. But unless the student has shown unmistakable talent and even originality as a performer, and is possessed of at least average health and strength, he or she is strongly recommended not to refuse, at all events at the start, any pupils who may happen to turn up whilst waiting for concert engagements. Making a living by concert playing is very attractive in prospect, but rarely profitable in fact, except, as before mentioned, in the case of those who are exceptionally gifted. There is no reason, however, why students should not combine both methods up to a certain point, and as circumstances permit.

The manner in which a young violinist establishes the beginning of a connexion varies accordingly as the work obtained is local or extraneous. As I am using these terms in a somewhat arbitrary sense I shall proceed to define them.

By local work I mean that which is done in the neighbourhood in which the student has grown up and perhaps been wholly or partially educated. Extraneous work is that to which he comes without introduction or influence other than that of such natural fitness and acquired experience as he possesses, and in performance of which he stands or falls by personal qualities only.

Local work has its advantages and disadvantages. The fact of one's family possessing a certain amount of influence through rank, political or class fellowship, or even through mere force of appeal to the feelings, as in the case of a widow's children, etc., is at once a benefit and a snare to the beginner, because, while it induces sundry persons to employ his or her services from motives other than that of simply acquiring the most suitable teacher or performer, it affects other persons in an exactly opposite manner, as they feel so familiar with the details of the student's career and personality as to have hardly that respect for his tutorial dignity which they would, perhaps unthinkingly, accord to a stranger.

It sometimes happens that the student obtains young or backward pupils through the agency of the School or College of Music in which he has graduated. They come to him with the understanding, spoken or implied, that they are to be passed on as soon as competent to the larger institution. This is an excellent arrangement as a start, and until the whilom student begins to develop original ideas on methods of teaching, or even to wish to experiment, with a view to selection from several methods. Then it begins, perhaps, to be awkward. The parent school clucks like an excellent hen over her duckling's aquatic exploits. If he swims, well and good; but if he happens to flounder in his first essay, then, heaven help him when he comes tamely ashore, within reach of remonstrant wings! The smaller and more provincial the institution, the more likely those connected with it are to resent any departure from its accepted canons, and for this reason the connexion, if prolonged, may come to be a shackle instead of a support to an aspiring scholar.

Now and then the first pupil arrives somewhat on this wise—most commonly to a girl student.

The father of the pupil in prospect has been a friend of her father's, now deceased, and he says, with a mixture of kindliness and complacency, that poor " So-

and-So's girl shall have *my* Jack and Joan at any rate, for the sake of old times.'' But he feels, very likely quite unconsciously, that under the circumstances his children have a prior claim on the attention and time of the teacher thus favoured. Even granting that this claim is to a great extent justified, it may possibly become a source of much further tribulation if the children in question happen to be backward or unruly, and do not make as good progress in the same time as those of less interested parents. Of course the teacher is not to blame for such a contretemps, but it behoves her to walk very warily between the Scylla of wounding really kindly feelings and the Charybdis of insincerely flattering or misleading powerful patrons. Of course, if the children are bright and promising, it will be a very pleasant task to repay goodwill with interest.

Another occasional drawback to purely local connexion is the likelihood of being asked to take certain pupils at especially cheap rates for reasons such as family friendships of long standing, business obligations, even denominational obligations ; which last are probably the most difficult of all to deal with.

A certain amount of this is almost unavoidable, and, indeed, not to be unduly bewailed ; but it sometimes reaches such a pitch as to seriously reduce the teacher's possible and legitimate earnings. This is peculiarly the case with performers who have indirectly become associated with religious or philanthropic societies. Philanthropic persons frequently seem to ignore the fact that the artists whom they requisition to assist at concerts in aid of this, that, or the other benevolent fund are possessed of quite as clamant human needs and necessities as the objects they are called upon to benefit. It is surely a topsy-turvy view of charity to dock a struggling violinist of half, or even the whole of his usual fee in order to bestow it upon persons or causes that may not be a whit more honestly in want of it if the facts were squarely faced. No artist would refuse his aid—nay, would proffer it most generously—if these appeals were restricted to such cases as bore upon the face of things a claim upon his humanity; but it is when concession becomes abused to the extent of common practice,—when not charity, but charity's hapless victim " suffereth long and is kind "—that one begins to look about and ask oneself whether it is not high time that these well-meaning blunderers should be taught to look at the matter from a more sane and sensible standpoint.

This last, though we have classed it with difficulties attached to local connexion, really crops up under extraneous circumstances quite as freely and embarrassingly, as the getters-up of charitable concerts think they are doing a favour by giving a young artist a chance to be heard by the public he wishes to reach. This persuasion has some seed of truth in it, but it should not be imagined to constitute a permanent claim upon the services of anyone who is earning a difficult living by just such concert performances, as it makes it extremely difficult for the violinist to obtain his fair fee from those semi-professional and amateur musical societies which abound in any large town.

On the whole, an extraneous connexion, though slower and more difficult to establish, is much more satisfactory in the long run, as it is worked on purely business principles and not complicated with social obligations which the musician is in constant fear of jarring or interrupting. Misunderstandings and petty jealousies between pupils and the parents of pupils can be controlled and allayed more successfully if the umpire is an outsider than if he or she is known to be a friend on one side or the other, and a stranger can send in the quarter's account, when necessary, without any of the qualms and self-consciousness which sometimes paralyse a habitué of the house, and make him submit to loss and inconvenience rather than jeopardise the goodwill of an agreeable acquaintance.

M

ON SOME PROFESSIONAL DIFFICULTIES.

A S the previous article was mainly concerned with the trials and troubles which not uncommonly beset the violinist in his earliest efforts to establish a connexion, it may not be out of place, here, to deal with some of the difficulties which will continue, and even increase with the extension of that connexion.

One of these, which we have already lightly touched upon, is the probability of jealousy arising either between pupils or patrons, or between those of his (or her) own profession who, justifiably or otherwise, may consider that he is trenching on their preserves, or setting himself up to be something greater than his diplomas or accomplishments warrant.

When jealousy arises between pupils the parents are usually at the bottom of it. Mrs. Brown's child has got on much faster than Mrs. Smith's, because the former ensures that the practising shall be regular and conscientious. Mrs. Smith's child is perhaps just as bright, but there is no regularity in the home life, and no inward compulsion towards improvement because of the slackness of the moral atmosphere. Mrs. Smith is undesirous, or perhaps incapable of realising this, and assumes that, in some unexplained way, Mrs. Brown's child has received more, or better quality of teaching. After a period of veiled hostility towards the teacher, and of *sotto voce* hinting among common acquaintances that she is the victim of favouritism, etc., which naturally diffuses a vague feeling of distrust, she probably removes the child; whereupon the same thing happens again, in due course, under the second teacher.

There are a great many Mrs. Smiths in the world, and we can offer no universal satisfactory rule for dealing with them. The most we can proffer is a few hints what *not* to do under similar circumstances. *Don't* condescend to insincerity to save your purse. *Don't* visit on the child what is really the sin of the parent; and *don't* worry more than twenty-four hours when what is perhaps an inevitable rupture arrives. But it is not always inevitable. It may sometimes be averted by gaining a hold on the child's affections without losing her respect, and by tactful praise and encouragement of some one good point, or even promise of a point, which she possesses in excess of other students.

Tact is of as much value as talent to the junior teacher. Without it, the road to success bristles with thorns and thistles. But it has no virtue unless it is allied to sincerity. Flattery lays a trap for the utterer and inconsistency a hidden pit. Moreover, tact consists not so much in what you utter as in the time and manner in which you utter it. It is possible to tell even a Mrs. Smith that she is responsible for her child's backwardness if only you go about it in a wise way, and with a broader and more tolerant understanding of the situation than she, personally, possesses.

Just as much care and forethought is necessary in dealing with the various little occasions of discord which may arise between you and your brother musicians. All professional existence, unfortunately, is competitive; and it is unavoidable that one man's weal should be, comparatively, another man's woe in the matter of obtaining pupils or concert engagements. This is usually accepted as philosophically as most other trying conditions of our human struggle, but now and again somebody permits a small grievance to rankle till it become a big grudge, and predisposes him to do us all the mischief he can provided he can work it anonymously. Such ambushed enemies can and do work a great deal of harm, not alone to young teachers but even to those of long experience and standing. If at all possible, it is wiser to force them into the open—when detected; but such natures have a rat's instinct for cover.

Of everyday occurrence are the little difficulties which arise about priority on a programme; about the passing on of pupils to more experienced professors; about unfair, or what seems to us unfair concert notices.

A youth with his way to win has got to wrestle along with taut muscles and steadfast aim; but he need not unnecessarily thrust his elbows into his neighbour's ribs, nor be perpetually on the lookout for slights. It doesn't as a rule hinder anybody's career to yield courteous place to age—especially to age but poorly gifted and struggling. It doesn't take the very least bit of gilt off our own gingerbread to give fair praise to a fair and honest rival, nor thanks for offices well meant if not always just what we desire.

But now and again it happens that we are justified in asserting ourselves. Mr. Slowcoach has had a monopoly of New Town since he was young and slim and it was a one-street village, and has made a comfortable and unexacting living by teaching its youngsters how to play " Home, Sweet Home," and " Melodies for the Multitude," with six inches of bow on a seven-and-sixpenny fiddle for more years than he cares to remember. By and bye comes the railroad, and we with it; our bags swollen with new diplomas, and our heads with new ideas, new methods, new ambitions, all clamorous for opportunity. Slowcoach doesn't want us one bit. His methods are rusty and his music out of date, and he knows that to put himself in trim for the coming battle will mean a radical change in all his dear ease-loving habits, and, in short, will be a most infernal nuisance. So he gathers his cronies and neighbours at his back and stirs up a little-great pother against us :—We are of the wrong creed, theological or political, or both; nobody knows where we came from (being purposely blind),

or how we behaved ourselves while there ; we are young
(a grave fault), and inexperienced (a worse), and unwill-
ing to submit ourselves to the guidance of our elders and
betters. In short, we intrude inexcusably; and must
be made to feel our position.

We probably do feel it to be exceedingly uncomfortable for a time, but we have only to hold on long enough
to show that we are really made of sterling stuff and
it will accommodate itself surprisingly to our desires.
In twelve months' time we shall be feeling quite an
affectionate pity for poor worried Slowcoach, getting
up early o' mornings to practise, and turning his out-of-
date polkas and schottisches on to the dust heap to make
room for the new studies, new scales and sonatas, and
all to keep pace with us, who were aforetime slighted!
Indeed, we are on the high road to becoming most complacently conceited, if we are not pricked to remember
that one day we, too—we, the now conquering—may
unavoidably fall behind through no fault of our own, and
be like poor old Slowcoach, scratching dull brains and
tasking stiff fingers to keep up with the requirements of
a day that is no longer ours.

Let us succeed, then, by all means, and with all our
might, but without bitterness and without inflation.
The world to-day is for the young ; and before we deem
that we have matured we are of yesterday, finding the
pace tell, and beholding day by day new hills overtopping
our old Alps. Of course we do not believe this when
we are twenty-one. Heaven forbid that we should ! for
it is often only our untried faith and courage that carries
us home so proudly on the crest of the wave. But,
since we are, unaccountably, in preaching vein, let us
commend to the junior violinist with whom we have
travelled so long, knowledge not only of his instrument
and of the things that pertain to music, but of the
texture of the life that surrounds him, and in which, for
good or evil, he plays his individual part. Let him look
on with seeing eyes, beholding fruit in the sheathed bud
and drawing nourishment from the husks of adversity.

To possess oneself ; that is the ideal : not to be moved overmuch by praise or blame, nor to excess by wrath or pity ; enjoying the pleasant things of life with frank and full appreciation, and accepting the bitter with quietness and a mind open to experience. Perhaps it is not till we have known and felt the utmost that we are capable of that it becomes possible to us really to observe and appreciate life ; at once entering into it with zest and purpose, yet being sufficiently able to detach ourselves from the hindrance of circumstance to appraise events, qualities and emotions at their true value. But anyone can refuse, from his school-days upward, to accept false coin ;—sham friendships, worthless approval, empty professions ;—and it will be well for the man-that-is-to-be if he puts small faith in either praise or affection that is too easily profuse and extravagant in expression.

ON KEEPING GOOD COMPANY.

" BUT this," says the Junior Violinist, "is a matter altogether outside the province of violin playing. Is it not enough to tell us what we ought to play, and how we must play it, and what we ought to feel whilst playing it, but this fellow must needs finger our leisure also and choose our acquaintance, send us out with Such-an-one, to walk to Such-a-place,—'and, mind, no dallying by the way . . .'"

Go not so fast, friend Reader, for it has more to do with violin matters than you wot of, being concerned at first hand with that goodly company of musicians whose songs or sarabandes, sonatas or saltarelles, form the substance of our daily converse with our violins.

It matters greatly to our violin what company *he* keeps ; so much so that if he be degraded from the concourse of wits and nobles, monarchs of sound and masters of sweet melody to that of dullards, mediocrities, and counterfeiters of each other's feeble airs, it sometimes seems that he falls sick—distempered with dull ditties, hoarse-voiced, uncertain, and lacking in his former brilliancy.

And why, forsooth ? Because, as a man's mind is enriched by association with his nobler fellows, kindled by intellectual fire, broadened by philosophy and mellowed by the humane study of humanity, so the instrument that has responded grandly to the call of nobler music,—that has been attuned and tempered constantly in its entire gamut, leaving no possibility untried, unpractised, if condemned now to echo trivial phrases, limited in breadth and scope, monotonous in rhythm and tonality, confined

to one small tract in all the varied kingdom of sound,—
if it, in spiritual exile, sometimes gives out sighs and
jarring groans of discontent, as might a mansion, many-
chambered and untenanted, windily creak and groan
without the closed door of the one small upper room
where an aged keeper tends her single fire,—is it, then,
much matter for wonder ?

And if our little comrade be so greatly influenced and
so readily responsive to *his* company, what of us ? Are
we untouched by what we play—more or less content in
the society of musical *élite* or riff-raff ? Or have we
ever even realised that what we choose to play, as what
we choose to read, to admire, to make our goal, bears its
part, and perhaps no small one, in the making and
maintaining of the man ? Or perhaps we do not actively
choose at all, but accept what is given to us by our
teachers, directly or indirectly; or what is easily ap-
plauded by our set ; or what has gained academical
approval; make acquaintance with much music but
friendship with none, and so miss the one thing that
makes art, any art, humanly valuable.

We are not holding briefs for any group of greatest
masters. Reason lays admiration's tribute at many a
shrine that wins no warmer feeling. Friendship for the
human personality breathing in the music or the book is
as much a matter of instinctive preference as our feeling
for the man whose hand we grasp and whose voice we
welcome at our door. We know that Bach is a king,
and we accord him a throne—but not, perhaps, the chair
at the fireside ; or it may be that he is our dearest guest
and all the moderns stand upon the outer circle.

But be that as it may—if you have no natural affinity
for a particular order of musical composition don't, as
you value your soul, assume an unreal sympathy with
it. Assumption of any taste foreign to our nature
leads eventually to sterility, discontent, even disgust
with the whole order of the universe. Do you think
I exaggerate ? Have you never pretended to esteem
some person, or virtue, or pursuit more highly than

you felt, either because you thought it raised your credit in the world's eyes or for any reason less than truth, and if you consider the occasion fairly, did it not leave in your mind a sense of dissatisfaction, depression, and of staleness in all things proportionate to the extent of your simulation?

To take a concrete instance:—Have you ever, in your student days or after, sat through a violin recital of Bach or Beethoven, given by renowned artists, and felt your thoughts perpetually wandering and fetched them back with a jerk because you thought you ought to be possessed by the music, and yet in your heart you were bored, and wondered whether other people were bored likewise, or whether they really experienced the enthusiasm they expressed or only dissembled better than you; or, if they really felt it, why you remained unthrilled? Have you ever questioned such a condition, and felt the whole world smaller because you could not comfortably travel in your neighbour's rut?

But perhaps your neighbour has an excellent house, or wife, or children, yet you unhesitatingly prefer your own; why, then, should you feel impelled to desire his tastes or ape his preferences? And it is not that they are not good, for many dissimilar things are equally good, but nothing is good for you that is not inherent.

Herewith a reader says:—" But what about *acquired* tastes? And may not one *cultivate* a taste for good music?"

"Acquired" tastes, taking the word literally, are in the writer's judgment, of indifferent value either as developing agents or mere aids to personal enjoyment. In the first case they presuppose an expenditure of force in overcoming natural antipathy, or at the least apathy, which force might be much more profitably expended along lines of less resistance; and in the second, who is to determine the real value of the acquisition? Not you, because your proper instinct declines responsibility. Your Neighbour?—but he is not living your life, and how can his verdict compass a complete understanding of you? Now, a natural taste is its own justification because it ministers to a natural hunger.

The plea for cultivation of good taste is a different matter. You cultivate that which has already its seed or root in you. When you were a child you perhaps instinctively liked those airs which had clear rhythm, meaning and purpose, and were complete in themselves without extraneous suggestion. They satisfied some as yet undefined desire of your being. If your first violin teacher was wise, he saw that you heard none other than these pure and lucid melodies until your original bent was sufficiently strengthened and cultivated to unhesitatingly reject all that was mediocre and spiritless, whether it came in the guise of academic dryness or of vulgar insipidity. If you had the misfortune to fall into the hands of an indifferent teacher, he let you play and play, indiscriminately, musical platitudes and pot-boilers until your first fine instinct was dulled and shaken and finally perished for lack of food, and you become one of that crowd which follows at the capricious heels of fashion, having neither the wit to challenge nor the courage to break away.

Cultivation, then, is not so much an intellectual courtesy as a moral duty. We come into the world with just so much individual power of adding to the intelligence, richness, or endurance of the life round us, and we have no other conceivable reason for existing than to develop that seed of power to the utmost.

But if we are at all able to judge of ourselves and to weigh our possibilities, we shall soon find that the same expenditure of mental force carries us much farther in some directions than in others, and that we willingly endure discomfort and fatigue in the pursuit of our best-desired attainment which would seem an intolerable burden were it otherwise directed.

Let us suppose, for instance, that a violinist who could have spent many hours with uplifting of spirit in the study of, perhaps Max Bruch's "Romanza" (Op. 42), is condemned to study instead, for the same period, unmitigated Hubay, or Paganini, or de Bériot. His practising immediately becomes a task, and he will have gained less even of technical proficiency at the end of the time and none of the mental refreshment, because he is working against the grain.

This does not apply to the practising of purely technical studies which is often, in a sense, against the grain, but from which one naturally does not expect to receive any intellectual gratification; nor does it preclude the becoming acquainted with very varied styles of composition so long as one does not spend undue time and energy upon any which do not afford the individual violinist sufficient genuine interest to repay his labour. On the other hand, the splendid challenge of those clarion thirds with which the *Piu Lento* of the "Romanze" opens calls up the finest feelings of our nature; the music is reinforced by all that we reverence most in poetry, in nature, in humanity, and we are better intellectually, morally, even physically for our noble company. Such is the true "communion of saints" if one divests the word of narrow theological significance, and holds the finest flower of thought and deed the world has known to be just sainthood. Supreme poets, painters, martyrs have, each one, given of their best; have only done with all their strength that which their inward self commanded them to do, and so have justified themselves. We of the rank and file may yet come near enough, if we desire, to share their spiritual atmosphere, to be refined and strengthened by that intermingled current of imperishable thought which sets into eternity.

The same composers will not have the same message for all men, but all music that is worthy of the name must possess in some degree similar enkindling and refining qualities; and by no means to be despised is the clean and wholesome merriment of Joseph Haydn, Boccherini, and, not least, Edward German. Life has room and reason for everything and symbols of everything; let us but see that we choose in each the best of its kind, stamped honest stuff, not shoddy.

Printed in Great Britain
by Amazon

21380588R00109